All About Pruning

Created and
designed by the
editorial staff
of ORTHO Books

Basic text
and research by
Charles Deaton
Michael MacCaskey

Art Direction by
Linda Hinrichs

Designed by
Jackie Jones

Illustrations by
Ron Hildebrand

Photography by
John Blaustein
Michael Landis
Wolf von dem Bussche

Ortho Books

Publisher
Robert L. Iacopi

Editorial Director
Min S. Yee

Managing Editors
Anne Coolman
Michael D. Smith
Sally W. Smith

Production Manager
Ernie S. Tasaki

Editors
Jim Beley
Susan Lammers
Deni Stein

Design Coordinator
Darcie S. Furlan

System Managers
Christopher Banks
Mark Zielinski

Photographic Director
Alan Copeland

Photographers
Laurie A. Black
Richard A. Christman

Production Editors
Linda Bouchard
Alice Mace
Kate O'Keeffe

Asst. System Manager
William F. Yusavage

Chief Copy Editor
Rebecca Pepper

Photo Editors
Anne Dickson-Pederson
Pam Peirce

National Sales Manager
Garry P. Wellman

Sales Associate
Susan B. Boyle

Operations Director
William T. Pletcher

Operations Assistant
Gail L. Davis

Administrative Assistant
Georgiann Wright

Address all inquiries to
Ortho Books
Chevron Chemical Company
Consumer Products Division
575 Market Street
San Francisco, CA 94105

First Printing in August, 1978

16 17 18 19 20 21
88 89 90 91 92 93

ISBN 0-917102-73-8

Library of Congress Catalog Card
Number 78-57891

Chevron Chemical Company
575 Market Street, San Francisco, CA 94105

Consultants
Robert Cannard
Horticulturist
Sonoma, CA

William Flemer III
President
Princeton Nurseries
Princeton, NJ

John Ford
Curator
Secrest Arboretum
Wooster, OH

Fred Galle
Director of Horticulture
Callaway Gardens
Pine Mountain, GA

Richard Hildreth
Director
State Arboretum of Utah
Salt Lake City, UT

Graphic Production
Jonson Pederson
Hinrichs & Shakery
San Francisco, CA

Copy Editing
Shirley Manning
Robert Bander

Typography
Terry Robinson & Co.
San Francisco, CA

Color Separations
Color Tech Corp.
Redwood City, CA

Photography
William Aplin: 32, 33, 34, 36, 37, 39, 42, 43

Marilyn Baker, 69

John Blaustein: Front Cover, 15, 18, 30, 32, 36, 40, 43, 57, 58, 68

John Bryan: 6, 85, 89

Walter Chandoa: 29, 49, 50, 51

Clyde Childress: 35, 41

Michael Landis: 21–23, 30, 31, 34, 36–38, 41–43, 50, 51, 53, 57–59, 61, 63, 72, 73, Back Cover

Michael MacCaskey: 35, 62

James K. McNair: 88, 89

Wolf von dem Bussche: 1, 4, 5, 10, 12, 17, 24, 25, 31, 32, 35, 38–40, 44, 62–65, 84

Min S. Yee: 30, 32, 34, 39, 41, 43, 56

Ortho Photo Library: 33, 36–40, 48–52, 56, 59–61, 63, 74–81

All About
Pruning

Why Prune?

Pruning can be as easy as rearranging the furniture in your own room. Try thinking of the outside of your house as you do the inside. When gardening, think of yourself as exterior decorator.

The history of pruning is as old as the history of civilized man. From the vast misty mountains of ancient China and the bas reliefs in Egypt's Valley of the Kings to the simple vineyards and orchards of the Holy Land and the tranquil gardens of Japan, each ancient civilization developed its own unique styles of pruning.

The ancient Chinese wanted to bring the distant mountains into their gardens, so they transported the naturally dwarfed plants they found in their highest mountains to their gardens. Later, this idea was introduced in Japan in the 13th and 14th centuries, and the idea became the exquisite art form we know today as bonsai. In fact, the pruning-for-voids in bonsai is the very essence of East Asian shape and feeling.

In Western civilization, the geometric design dominated. The bas reliefs on the tombs of the pharaohs depict plants pruned much as we prune geometric shapes into our espaliers both here in the United States and in Europe today.

However, the most basic instructions for pruning for food came from the Bible. The Hebrew lawbook Leviticus says, "Six years you shall sow your field and six years you shall prune your vineyard, and gather in its fruit." Isaiah, in one of the most eloquent passages in history, admonishes, "And they shall beat their swords into plowshares and their spears into pruning hooks." And in the New Testament, from the Book of John, we find these pruning instructions: "I am the true vine and my Father is the vinedresser. Every branch of mine that bears no fruit he takes away, and every branch that does bear fruit, he prunes that it may bear more fruit."

The Roman historian Pliny wrote of the man who must plant first for his god, then for his heirs and lastly for himself, with pruning to guarantee the results. Actually, the Greeks and the Romans followed the Egyptians' lead, with potted plants shaped into formal topiaries for use inside their homes and outside on patios. Eventually, this practice spread throughout the Roman Empire and resulted in the formal parterre gardens at Versailles and the controlled informal English treatment of gardens during the 15th and 16th centuries.

In America, the early gardens —

Left: The trees and shrubs of historic Williamsburg show the results of careful attention to pruning. The American elm in the background has received regular corrective pruning to prolong its life. The maple in the foreground frames the house beautifully.

Right: Think of yourself as an exterior decorator, in which the planting to the front is like the carpet; the shrubs, walls and trees are the ceiling.

such as George Washington's at Mount Vernon and Thomas Jefferson's at Monticello — reflect this influence in the formal box hedges and the use of native plants trimmed in an English style.

Today, pruning is as necessary as ever if we are to maintain order in our gardens and increase the fruits of our labors. In fact, the definition of a garden could well be "a place that has been pruned for the benefit of both plants and persons."

And so, there are no mysteries about pruning. It is a horticultural practice that is as ancient as the cradles of civilization. It is a heritage, a wonderful heritage, that has been left to us all.

In this book, we are merely trying to pass on some of what we have learned.

If you feel that pruning is a mysterious art best left to professionals, read on in this book. It will change your mind about needing to hire someone to control that jungle of vegetation that seems to be crawling toward your house.

Actually, pruning can be as uncomplicated as rearranging the furniture in a room. There are only a few basic plant shapes to keep in mind. And you can snip a branch as confidently as you move a lamp. How? By understanding the simple principles of how plants grow. Once you learn to meet your plants' simple needs, you'll discover that pruning pays both practical and esthetic dividends.

A good definition of pruning is: *the removal of part of a plant for the benefit of all the plant.* Pruning has three basic effects: it *directs growth,* it *improves health* and it *increases production.*

Let's consider each of these points in turn.

The benefits of pruning

Pruning directs growth
This can be an esthetic benefit of pruning. But it's also a practical one if you want to bring a lopsided tree into balance to prevent its uneven weight from breaking it. Of course, you can also prune to keep a tree small, to have it grow slim and taller or to open it up by thinning it out.

Pruning to direct growth is also a way to control the microclimate of your garden. The cuts you make can affect the movement of air, the degree of sunlight and shade entering a yard, air temperature — even the condition of the soil.

Growth itself is another basic plant response to pruning. Pruning can rejuvenate an old, sparse shrub or tree.

Pruning improves health
Consider an apple tree as an example. Opening up the inside of the tree allows more air to circulate and more sun to penetrate to the innermost leaves. With the exception of spraying, this is the best possible way to prevent disease, and is preferable to excessive spraying.

To insure a healthy transplant is another reason for pruning. It reduces the number of leaves on transplanted plants to compensate for root loss and thus reestablishes the necessary leaf/root ratio.

Pruning can also keep a plant healthy by correcting or repairing damage. Removing a dead and possibly diseased branch can keep the infection from spreading to healthy wood.

Pruning increases production
If we prune that same apple tree correctly, its crop will improve. In general, the more branches the tree has, the greater the number of apples. Reduce the number of branches and those that remain will bear larger apples.

Plants vary in their need for pruning. Some need lots every year; some need only a little in a lifetime; some never need it unless they are injured.

Later we describe *if, how* and *when* you should prune specific plants. But before getting into these details, stand back for a moment and consider your garden as a whole.

The gardener as exterior decorator
Try thinking of the *out*side of your house as you do the *in*side. Then you'll find that decisions about what and how much to prune are easier to make.

Think of a garden as having green walls or screens. Hedges are exactly that: living, leafy walls along the edge of each main space.

Against this background shrubs are placed, like furniture. Some shrubs are covered with flowers, as bright and cheerful as the floral coverings on sofas and easy chairs.

Vines are natural substitutes for drapes, cascading down fences and walls. And, of course, the carpet for your garden room can be smooth green grass or something more colorful and textured, like bugleweed *(Ajuga)* or another flowering ground cover.

Tree trunks are strong columns supporting leafy ceilings that enclose the garden room.

If you keep this indoor/outdoor comparison in mind, it will be easier to maintain an attractive garden. Once you visualize that tangle of greenery simplified into a few forms, you'll see how to keep those forms neat and trim.

Heading Back

Heading back keeps the plant denser and sturdier. It creates a more formal looking plant. However, headed trees tend to force many weakly attached, vigorous upright shoots, and may change the tree's natural shape. As the illustration above shows, to head back you simply cut around the entire shape. In general, heading back is more applicable to hedges than to trees.

Thinning

Thinning a plant — that is, taking out whole branches — produces a taller, more open plant with a natural individual grace. This is the way to train a plant to appear more natural looking.

Six Styles of Pruning

There are only six basic forms to distinguish and any of them can be pruned to look either formal or natural — the choice is yours:

Hedges define garden space, raising green walls of privacy from the world outside; they can create vistas within the garden or separate one area from another. For instance, a hedge can section off a large central lawn from a children's play space. Hedges can look either formal or natural. Shave the sides flat, give them flat tops, and you'll have a crisp, formal wall. Let them grow more irregularly and the effect will be loose and natural. *(See pages 53-63.)*

Shrubs are the largest space fillers in the garden. Group the highest shrubs farthest back, the lowest always in the foreground so that you can see each shrub's particular texture and color play against all the others. Shrubs, like hedges, can be pruned to look formal or natural. *(See pages 53-73.)*

Borders divide shrubs and flowers from flat garden space. A border could be an 8-inch tall boxwood *(Buxus)* separating flowering shrubbery from the lawn, edging the brick path or surrounding the paved patio. You may recall pictures of French gardens with patterns formed of boxwood borders, the sides severely clipped at right angles to the top. If you let boxwood grow more naturally, with rounded sides and irregularly mounded tops, you'll have an English garden. Pruning sets the style. *(See page 55.)*

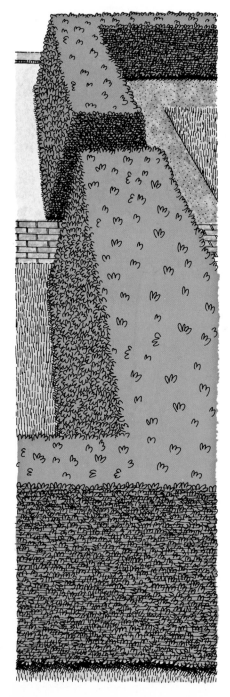

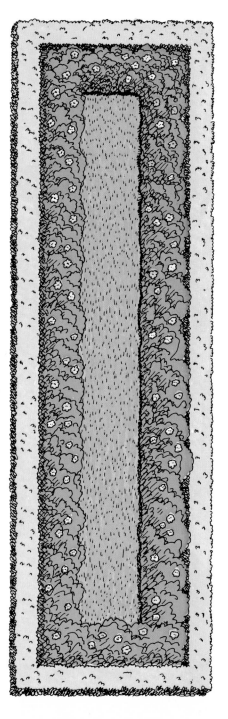

Vines can drape and soften walls with gently fluttering green or colorful blooms. They can be left to sprawl naturally or be trained in formal patterns; for example, ivy grown in diamond lines on a brick wall. *(See pages 75-83.)*

Topiary is garden sculpture comparable to an indoor accent piece. By shaping plants into geometric and animal forms, you can give your yard a fanciful touch. Although a boxwood obelisk is unnatural, it's hard to beat as a dramatic green sculpture. Would you like a lion as the focal point? Carve him out of greenery and you'll have a king of the jungle who requires only a little plant food and water.

Now that you've read about the visual effects you can gain by pruning, what about the plants themselves? How do you make pruning decisions based on what's good for a plant? *(See pages 85-89.)*

Trees are the strongest architectural lines in a garden. They add height to the garden and also determine whether its floor will be bright with cheerful flowers or a shaded refuge from the sun. *(See pages 23-43.)*

A few principles of shaping

As you study the guidelines that we give later in this book for pruning specific plants, you'll notice that they reduce to a few common principles:

☐ Pruning can either dwarf a plant or make it grow taller.

☐ Heading back a plant (reducing its size) keeps the plant denser and sturdier. Heading back will create a more formal looking plant.

☐ Thinning the plant — that is, taking out whole branches — produces a taller, more open plant with a natural individual grace. This is the way to train a plant to look more natural.

☐ As a tree matures, the increasing thickness of branches makes them appear to grow closer together on the trunk but their spacing actually remains the same. For example, if you carve your initials on a tree, they will remain at exactly the same height as you carved them, even though the tree may grow another 5 feet or even 50 feet.

☐ Strong light produces a thick growth of leaves, limbs, flowers and fruit. Weak light usually produces thinner growth, fewer flowers and less fruit.

☐ Two branches growing close together are in competition. If you shorten one, its longer neighbor will mature more readily.

We have tried to organize this book so that the material will be as accessible as possible. If you read on in the text and discover that you've forgotten what an "adventitious bud" is, thumb quickly to the back of the book and look it up in our illustrated glossary. Specific plants can be found by both their botanical and common names in the general index at the end of the book.

Use the plant as your guide

Following in this book are many words about pruning. You'll find the information is accurate but by its nature, generalized. For that reason, we ask you not to forget that each type of plant has individual characteristics that may vary from garden to garden. Use this book to get started, then let the plant being pruned be the teacher.

Below:
English yews (Taxus baccata) are widely planted topiary and hedge plants. They grow so slowly that formal, neat shapes are retained with only annual shearing. Use varieties of T. media in colder regions.

Right: Well-pruned trees with open branch patterns provide beauty, shade and the coolness of natural air-conditioning.

Pruning's Simple Rules

The most bewildering questions for the beginner
are: "When do you prune?" and "Where do you cut?"

A plant's parts

A pruner needs to know something
about the basic parts of a plant: roots,
stem or trunk, branches, leaves, flowers and fruits. Fortunately, the parts
of all plants are the same, even though
they don't always look alike from plant
to plant.

Roots

In the case of roots, nature provides
a not uncommon example of a single
part functioning in more than one way.
Roots serve two major purposes: they
anchor the plant and they absorb
water and necessary mineral nutrients.

Stem or trunk

You can think of this part of the plant
as a pair of plumbing pipes, one inside the other, wrapped in bark. The
inner pipe carries water and minerals
from the roots up to the branches,
leaves, flowers and fruit. The outer
pipe carries food down from the leaves
to the rest of the plant. Another function of the stem or trunk is obviously
the support of branches, leaves, flowers and fruit.

Branches

As the trunk supports the branches,
they in turn serve as a framework
for the leaves. Branches are named
according to their positions on the
trunk. The *leader* is the central, highest branch, seemingly a continuation
of the trunk itself. *Scaffold* branches
are the main side branches. *Lateral*
branches emerge horizontally from
scaffold limbs. *Hangers* are lateral
fruit-tree branches that drop after bearing the weight of the previous year's

*The basic framework of a tree
consists of the trunk and scaffold
or main branches. Scaffold
branches should be well-spaced
with wide angles of attachment
in order to have a healthy,
mature tree.*

Basic Anatomy of a Tree

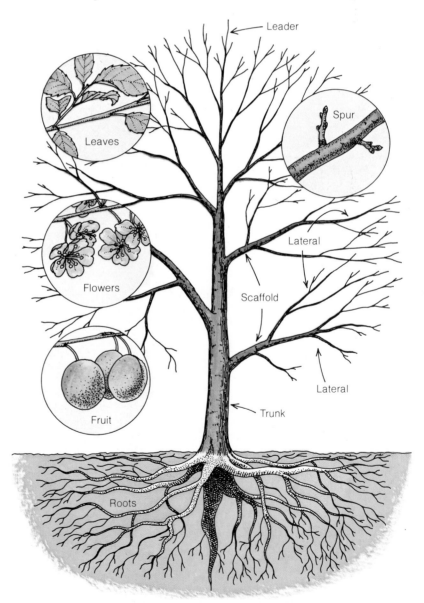

Leader

Spur

Leaves

Lateral

Flowers

Scaffold

Fruit

Lateral

Trunk

Roots

crop; the same word is used for unnaturally drooping branches and for broken branches that hang up in the tree and pose a safety threat. *Spurs* are the short twigs or branchlets that bear flowers and fruit. *Suckers* are leafy shoots that sprout at a tree's crown or from its roots. Because they may rob the plant of nutrients and water, they normally should be removed. *Water sprouts* are shoots that grow above the pruned parts of a tree.

Leaves

Food is manufactured mainly in the leaves by the sun. The process of photosynthesis creates carbohydrates through the action of chlorophyll in the leaves combined with the energy of the sun.

Flowers and fruits

Flowers are the sexual portion of plants that produce seeds for reproduction.

When do you prune?

This is probably the most bewildering question for the beginner — although one friend of ours, a horticultural professor, advises succinctly: "Prune when your shears are sharp." Is the best time in winter or spring, before flowering or after?

To answer this question, you need to know: (1) when the plant flowers and (2) on which of three kinds of growth it flowers — shoots from the current season, wood from the previous year, or wood two or more years old.

Shoots from the current season

There's a good reason for pruning all plants that bloom on new shoots *before* the plants bloom. Consider roses as an example. Most rose flowers are initiated on shoots grown during the current year. Pruning them in the spring before they begin to bloom will encourage new growth and more roses.

Wood from the previous year

Many plants, such as forsythia, bloom on year-old wood. Prune these plants *after* flowering. If you prune year-old wood in the spring, you prune away flowering wood. If you should cut away *all* of last year's wood, there would be no flowers at all this year.

Wood two or more years old

An apple tree flowers on wood several

The stem is a 2-way street

Water and minerals come up through the stem into all plant parts above the ground. Food from the leaves goes down to the roots.

A close-up look

Once you become familiar with the names and placement of these smaller plant parts you will recognize them from plant to plant, and from stem to stem.

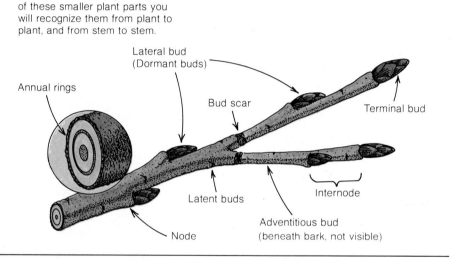

Annual rings

Lateral bud (Dormant buds)

Bud scar

Terminal bud

Latent buds

Internode

Adventitious bud (beneath bark, not visible)

Node

The bud's growth cycle

Dormant buds have a great deal of potential.

Vegetative buds contain embryonic leaves and branches . . .

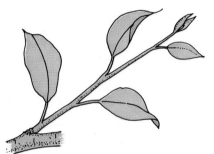

that will unfurl and grow.

Some contain rudimentary flowers as well as leaves and branches.

Flowers like these benefit pollinating insects and delight all who see them.

Fruits follow the flowers, and seeds signal the end of the cycle.

years old, so you don't have to be as selective in pruning it. Just cut to shorten and thus to strengthen the fruit-bearing branches.

As you can see, pruning is almost entirely based on common sense. If you remember when a plant flowers and on what kind of wood, you'll always know when to prune it.

Pinching is in-between pruning

After you have pruned a plant for the year, you can reduce the amount of pruning you will have to do the following year by a process called "pinching" — shortening the shoots you don't want for branches by pinching out the tips. Doing this diverts the plant's strength into the branches or buds you do want to develop. Leaves on the pinched or stubbed shoots will shade the trunk or stem of the plant and continue to manufacture food for the benefit of the whole plant.

Pinching creates denser growth and a more compact plant that may later require thinning.

Where do you cut?

Before leaves and new stems appear, they exist in small swellings on the stems and branches called "buds." Inside these buds wait tiny, undeveloped leaves, branches and flowers.

In spring, buds swell and lengthen into stems, unfurl into leaves and burst into flowers. The flowers produce fruit and then, when the fruit is almost ripe and seeds have formed, the growth in most plants stops.

From the very first swelling of buds, all of a mature plant's efforts go to producing seeds for the continuation of the species. Once this is done, the cycle of growth is complete. Although branches go on thickening and fruit sweetens and drops, no more leaves, flowers or fruit will appear until next spring. Soon leaves will fall from deciduous plants, and evergreen plants will become dormant.

Buds — terminal, lateral and flower

If you look closely at buds, you'll see that there are three main kinds: terminal, lateral and flower. A *terminal* bud grows at the tip of a shoot. Protected by bud scales, it is plump with a future branch. Another main type is called a *lateral* bud; it appears on the side of the shoot.

Usually, a fruit tree's *flower* buds are shorter, blunter and fatter than its vegetative (leaf-producing) buds. Flower buds appear on spurs on fruit trees and can be in either a terminal or lateral position on a vegetative shoot.

As shown in the mosaic of limbs and twigs of this Liriodendron tulipifera *(Tulip tree), the tree's structure becomes more apparent when leafless.*

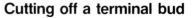

Choosing the right bud

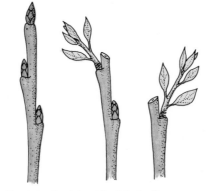

Prune by the lateral bud that will produce the branch you want. An outside bud will usually produce an outside branch. The placement of that bud on the stem points the direction of the new branch.

Cutting off a terminal bud

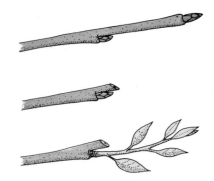

Generally, the strongest growth goes into the terminal bud. When you cut it, the closest lateral bud inherits its strength. In fact, that lateral bud becomes the new terminal bud.

The correct cut

Hold the branch below where the cut will be made. Put the cutting blade of your hand pruners under the branch. Cut at an upward angle. The slant of the cut should be in the direction you want the new branch to grow.

The way to cut close

One advantage of the scissors type of hand pruners is that you can cut closer to the trunk. Position the thin cutting blade on the trunk side of the cut. The resulting stub will then be as short as possible.

The pruning knife

To use a pruning knife requires both skill and a sharp blade. A blunt knife can damage the plant and, worse, slip and cut your hand. Keep your hand away from the direction of the cut and keep the blade sharpened on an oil stone.

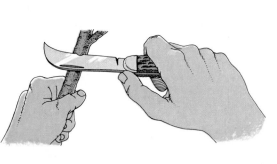

The 3-saw cut

This is the way to remove heavy branches without damaging the tree. The first cut [1] is made on the branch underside and the second cut [2] on the top and slightly farther out on the limb. The weight of the branch will cause the branch to fall and break off at the point where the bottom cut was made. This cutting sequence avoids having the bark tearing down the trunk of the tree. A rope is useful when removing the heaviest branches. The third and final cut [3] is made at the point shown in the illustration: either through the "growth rings" (dotted line) or at the points of the bisected angles.

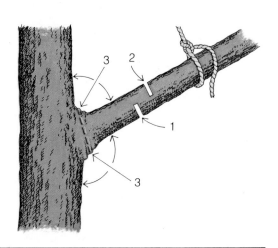

If all lateral buds grew at the same time, the plant would soon exhaust its ability to produce food and would topple from its weight. Most of these lateral buds, though, do not grow the first year. They are called *dormant* buds. If they remain dormant for more than one year, they are called *latent* buds.

There is still one other type — the *adventitious* bud. It usually remains dormant and will start into action only in response to an emergency to the plant, such as the removal of a limb.

The *node* is the juncture where a leaf or lateral bud joins the stem or branch. The part of the branch between nodes is called the *internode*.

On some stems that are two or three years old, you'll notice rings several inches apart. These are the *annual bud scar rings* that, on most trees, show the length of each year's growth.

Cut above the buds

When you prune, always cut just above a bud. Why? Consider what happens when you cut off a terminal bud just above a lateral bud. The terminal bud grows most strongly. The lateral bud that is now at the tip of the stem will inherit this strength. This is called *apical dominance*.

When you choose a lateral bud to place your cut, select one that is pointing outward so that the new branch produced by the bud will grow out from the trunk rather than criss-crossing with other branches inside the foliage. Cutting above an outward-pointing lateral bud will also open up the plant for light, air and orderly growth — important goals in pruning.

Let's choose a rose plant to illustrate these two points. A 6-foot grandiflora rose bush in front of a window might block the view. Without damaging or endangering the plant, you can prune it down to 4 feet and train it to grow wider and fuller.

To do this, first prune all the stems to a height of about 3 feet, cutting at outside lateral buds. Since the newly reduced bush will have fewer leaves, it cannot send as much food to the roots. In turn, the reduced roots can support less abundant foliage. As a result, the plant's branches will stay around 4 feet high during this year. Next year it will grow taller, but you can again trim it back.

These rules may seem simple enough, but it should also be kept in mind that *no cut should ever be made without a good reason and a clear understanding of what the results are likely to be.*

Beautifully manicured trees and shrubs backdrop the annual color planting at Filoli Center. a display garden in Woodside, Ca.

Tools and Techniques

Buying good tools is important. The quality of the steel determines the quality of the cut. But did you know that one of your most important tools will cost you nothing?

Tools of the trade

One of your most important pruning tools will cost you nothing; it consists of your thumb and forefinger. No other tool is better for pinching off tiny buds or leaf tips. The first tool to buy, though, is a pair of hand pruners. You will make most of the necessary cuts with this indispensable tool.

Hand pruners that can be used on wood up to ¾ inches thick are available in two main types. Scissor-style pruners have sharpened blades that overlap in making the cut. This type is liable to twist if forced, making a jagged, injurious cut. But, kept sharp and used properly, scissor-style pruners give a close, clean cut.

Anvil-style pruners have a sharpened top blade that snaps onto a flat plate of softer metal. Though lighter and easier to handle than the scissor type, this pruner always crushes the bark on the anvil side and cannot cut as close as the scissor type.

Lopping shears are pruners with long handles to give extra leverage when making cuts in wood up to 1¼ inches thick. Heavy-duty loppers are available for cutting through wood 1¾ inches thick.

Pruning saws are used for heavier work. They can cut wood that is 2 inches in diameter and up. Never force hand pruners or loppers to cut anything too thick. The smaller pruning saws have narrow, back-cutting teeth on a curved blade, handy for use in narrow spaces. Some saws have teeth

The back-cutting teeth of this type of pruning saw is preferred for pruning over the typical hand saws used in general carpentry. Also, size and shape of the saw allow for greater freedom of movement in areas where space is crowded by the presence of other branches.

on both sides, one for coarse cuts, one for fine cuts. The disadvantage of the double-edged saw is that when you're cutting with one side, the teeth on the other side may tear the bark of nearby limbs.

Wide blade saws are for the largest limbs. They're about the size of an ordinary carpenter's saw but some are curved. There are also saws with both cutting teeth and rakers, such as the Tuttle tooth saw.

Extension loppers and saws should be used if the branch is no more than 2 inches thick and is out of reach. You attach tools at the end of the extension pole and operate them by pulleys and ropes.

Hedge shears have long, scissor-like blades to trim and shape bushes. To prevent the foliage from slipping away, buy the kind of shears that has one blade notched. Because manual shears are tiring to use for long, you may want to buy electric hedge shears. These are faster, easier to use and allow greater accuracy of line.

Chain saws are designed to cut heavy tree branches. They are available in many sizes and models and may be gasoline, electric or even hydraulically powered. These are among the most common tools of the professional tree pruner. They can be rented if your use is infrequent. Climbing into a tree with a chain saw is extremely dangerous; we don't advocate it.

Pruning knives are used to smooth the rough edges on the trunk after making large cuts. Another handy tool for smoothing the edges of wounds is a wood rasp. We've experimented with rasps and found them somewhat easier to use than a knife.

Pinching

One of your most important pruning tools costs you nothing. It consists of your thumb and index finger.

Annuals and perennials — or, for that matter, anything you can break off with your fingers — will become more dense and bushier with new growth after pinching.

Tools

Hand Pruners

Use on stems up to ¾ inches in diameter. They come in two main types:
☐ Scissor-style pruners have sharpened blades that overlap in making the cut.
☐ Anvil-style pruners have a sharpened top blade that snaps onto a flat plate of softer metal. Though lighter and easier to handle than the scissor type, this pruner always crushes the bark on the anvil side and cannot cut as close as the scissor type.

Hedge shears

Use on all hedges except those with protruding stems over ½ inches in diameter. To prevent the foliage from slipping away, buy the kind that has one blade notched.

Pruning knife

Use to smooth the rough edges on the trunk or large branch after making a large cut. Smoothing the edges helps the tree heal more quickly.

Narrow curved pruning saw

Use on branches up to 2 inches in diameter where the branches are too densely crowded to effectively wield a wide blade saw.

Electric hedge shears

Use on all hedges except those with stems

protruding over ¾-inches in diameter. Because manual shears are tiring after prolonged use, the electric shears quickly become a welcome relief. They are faster, easier to use and allow greater accuracy of line.

Extension saw

Use on out-of-reach branches up to 2 inches in diameter. The curved blade operates like the narrow curved pruning saw.

Wide blade saw

Use on the largest limbs. The forward-angled teeth work like a carpenter's saw.

Double-edged saw

Use on larger branches. One side of this saw has small teeth that cut when the saw is pushed, and is used for small branches and deadwood. The other side has coarse teeth that cut larger branches on both strokes.

Lopping shears

Use on branches up to 1¼ inches in diameter. Heavy duty loppers are available for cutting through wood 1¾ inches thick.

Chain saw

Use on branches over 3 inches in diameter. Although chain saws eliminate much hard work, they should be operated very carefully.

Wood rasp

Use to smooth the rough edges on the trunk or large branch after making a large cut. Many people found the wood rasp somewhat easier to use than a pruning knife.

Extension loppers

Use on out-of-reach branches that are no more than 2 inches thick.

Choosing and caring for tools

Buying good tools is important. The quality of the steel in the cutting edges of pruning tools determines the quality of the cuts. If tools have strong working parts, they will last. Good tools also have a way of turning work into pleasure. Don't look for bargains. Cheap tools cost more in the long run.

Keeping tools sharp and clean will make your work easier. Dry the blades of your tools after each use and prevent rust by rubbing them with a few drops of oil; put some on the joints, too. If shears tear plants when you cut, you can usually tighten the tool. If not, it may have sprung and you might as well throw it away.

Good quality shears rarely get out of alignment. When they do, it's because they've been used on larger branches than they were designed to cut.

A clear picture

Before you prune, you should always have a clear picture in mind of how you would like to have the finished plant look.

The order of cuts

The typical sequence to follow when pruning any plant is: first, remove any dead, diseased, misplaced or criss-crossing branches. Then begin thinking of improving or enhancing the form of the plant. Usually, make the smallest cuts first, gradually working toward removal of larger limbs.

Cutting small stems and shoots. Use pruning shears to make the smallest cuts and, remember, always cut just above a healthy lateral bud. Cut at ¼ inch above the bud from which you want a branch to grow. If you cut too far from the bud — say, over an inch — the whole stem may die back. If you cut too close to the bud, you will kill it. Slant the cut upward toward the top of the bud, with the angle in the direction you want the new branch to grow.

To develop a new branch that will grow outward, cut above an outside bud. In that rare instance when you want a branch to grow inward — usually to fill a vacant space — cut just above a bud pointed in that direction.

Cutting small branches. Use lopping shears for branches that measure up to 1¼ inches thick. Make the cuts exactly as you would with hand pruners.

Cutting larger branches. Any branch up to about 3 inches in dia-

meter can be cut with a hand saw or, if you prefer, a chain saw. A branch too heavy to hold with your free hand should be stubbed off about 6 inches from the trunk before you make the finished cut next to the trunk. This precaution prevents the bark from being stripped from the trunk if the heavy branch should slip from your hand before you've finished the cut.

Cutting big limbs. Use a wide blade, single-edged saw for branches over 3 or 4 inches thick. Use a 3-legged pruning ladder to reach high branches; it's the most stable kind of ladder. As a precaution, tie the top of the ladder to a nearby branch.

When your ladder is secure, cut off all side branches from the limb to be removed. This is necessary for two reasons: (1) the weight of all those branchlets and leaves makes your main pruning job much more difficult, and (2) a branch that falls through the tree with side branches still attached can damage other branches on its way down. Very heavy branches can be further lightened by removing a section at a time. Cutting off sections of a heavy limb one by one is often the only safe way to handle the biggest branches.

The 3-saw cut. After you've trimmed off the side branches, protect the trunk's bark by making a shallow cut at the underside of the limb where it's attached to the trunk. If the limb is long, remove it in two or three cuts, leaving a section of 2 or 3 feet attached to the trunk. Before you make the first cut, tie a rope around the outer section of the limb and attach the rope to a higher branch. After you've made the cut, lower that section to the ground. Then retie the rope to the remaining section(s) and make the final cuts.

Wound healing

To help a plant heal properly from a pruning wound, use a wood rasp or a pruning knife to clean off any jagged edges. The smoother the cut surface, the faster it will heal.

If you make the cut as smooth as possible — especially at the cambium layer (where the bark connects to the wood) — this will aid the development and fast growth of callus, which the tree uses to compartmentalize the wound.

The shape of the wound is not critical.

Experts will disagree about a lot of things in pruning. Get ten into a garden and you'll have ten different opinions on how to keep a particular tree or shrub healthy and shapely. However, most experts support the general principle of letting nature have her way as much as possible.

Snap cut gear pruners

This type of multi-powered gear driven pruner allows one to cut dead wood, roots and branches up to 1¼ inches in diameter. They have three times as much cutting power as the conventional lopping shears of the same size. The cut shown above should now be finished by smoothing with a pruning knife, wood rasp, or small saw. A smooth finish promotes formation of healing callus tissue.

Pneumatic shears

This air-powered shears is being used for commercial pruning of muscadine grapes.

Ornamental Trees

An encyclopedic guide to more than 100 species of the most commonly planted trees. What are the growth characteristics of a specific tree? How do you prune? When do you prune?

Pruning young trees

A young tree just brought from the nursery may have a trunk not much thicker than its few skinny, short branches. It requires special and prompt pruning.

Resist the temptation to preserve every leaf in order to have the tree grow larger as quickly as possible. You must make several important cuts at planting. The earlier the shaping, the less major pruning it will need in later years.

It's a good idea, too, when you are planting a tree to place some long-acting controlled-release fertilizer at the bottom of the planting hole; see the manufacturer's directions for amount of fertilizer to use. This is one time when it is easy to get phosphorus underneath a tree. This type of fertilizer does not move down through the soil as easily as nitrogen does. And add an organic soil amendment to your back fill, blending it well before shoveling it into the planting hole.

Deciduous trees that lose their leaves are usually sold with bare roots during their first winter or in early spring. The ornamental flowering crabapple is an example.

Pruning a newly planted tree should have the effect of balancing the root and top systems. Some roots are inevitably lost when a tree is transplanted. If the nursery hasn't already done so, you should immediately remove some

Left: The Ginkgo biloba *usually forms a strong central leader with wide-angled, dramatically radiating branches. Its' fall color is a brilliant yellow.*

Right: This eye-catching tree is a native of the Pacific Northwest. Left to nature's own pruning, Prunus emarginata *(Bitter plum) developed a beautiful form with three central leaders.*

Before pruning

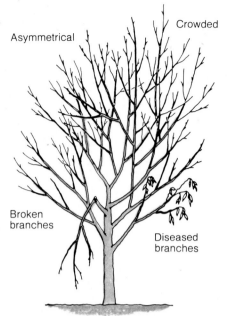

Asymmetrical
Crowded
Broken branches
Diseased branches

Above is shown the most typical needs of an unpruned tree: crowded foliage, asymmetrical shape, broken and diseased branches. Other reasons for pruning include controlling size and increasing the amount of sunlight to a window or to plants in the shade of the tree.

After pruning

If you regularly prune to remove broken, diseased, crossing and asymmetrical (or out-of-place) branches, then you will reduce future problems and have a healthy, attractive tree.

of the top growth to compensate for this root loss and to provide a stronger frame for future growth. The top doesn't have to be made smaller: just thin out the weaker or crossing branches to reduce the total leaf area. Be sure also to remove any fruit that might develop the first year.

The ideal ornamental tree has a straight tapered trunk and balanced shape with scaffold branches emerging from the trunk at a 45° angle. Generally, branches that angle up too closely to the tree trunk produce a weak crotch that will become weaker each year. The wider the angle of a scaffold branch, the stronger it becomes.

Look at your young tree carefully. Identify the leader first, then 2 or 4 primary branches. These branches will become main scaffold branches. Cut them back to an outward facing bud so that they are not as tall as the leader.

Another important thing to know about leaders is that if two leaders are left, the result will be a forked-leader tree — a tree with two trunks. Unless the tree is a multistemmed type in its natural form, trouble arises when the trunks grow together and, sooner or later, one becomes weaker and possibly splits away. Only major tree surgery can then restore the tree. Even so, the remaining trunk is usually so unbalanced that it may topple in a storm.

If you've bought a tree in a container and its root system has been pruned or damaged during transplanting, estimate the amount of root loss and then cut or thin the top accordingly. Although this may seem like excessive cutting, it is essential for the strength and health of the future tree. The branch stubs that remain will grow thicker and stronger, receiving all the food the longer branches would have taken. In addition, the fewer buds that remain on the branches will produce more shoots.

Careful pruning of a young tree will help it develop a strong structure, survive disease and misfortunes, and grow to a picturesque old age.

After you have pruned to balance roots and leaves and to form the basic structure, you can let the tree grow until next year, except for light summer pruning.

Second pruning

The second year's pruning is often the most important one in the life of the tree. Why? Because a young tree planted in rich, properly watered soil will usually respond extravagantly, producing heavy bunches of new shoots and foliage. If the heavy branches are left alone they tend to sag from their weight and may even

break. You must cut off some of this weight. You can do it in two ways, depending on the kind of tree shape you want to form.

If you want a wide and airy tree with much open space, leave the terminal shoot on the primary branches and eliminate most of the lateral shoots. This reduces the weight but retains the length of the branches, directing future growth farther outward.

If you want a strong and compact tree, cut the terminals back to a side shoot on each branch. This shortened branch will become stronger and the tree will grow in a more compact shape.

The scaffold branches may have become as high as or higher than your selected leader during the year's growth. Since they will compete with the leader, they must be cut back again below the height of the leader. You should repeat this for the first five or ten years until the general shape of the tree is established.

It's important to keep in mind the function of the tree in your landscape. Are you setting off an attractive view or screening out an unsightly one? Do you want branches invitingly low for children to climb or a high canopy for shading the house? It's much easier to accentuate the natural form of a young tree than to force a new function on a mature tree.

Third and fourth prunings

During the third and fourth years in the life of a tree, its scaffold branches require your attention.

As the tree grows taller, you'll have to select scaffold branches from among the numerous candidates produced higher on the tree. Choose carefully. Select each scaffold branch from around the tree so that air and light will freely reach the leaves on its lateral branches. The spacing will vary from 8 or 12 inches for the slight Japanese maple to 24 or 36 inches for a large oak.

Continue to keep weight from accumulating on these branches, selecting only shoots that help the framework and eliminating all others. Tip the shoots that you wish to shorten, making the cut just beyond a bud pointing in the desired up and out direction.

Pruning your tree while it is young is the very best way to make sure it will grow into the shape you want. If large branches are cut off later, the resulting large wound may open the tree to infection. Young trees are usually less susceptible to infection than old trees — another reason to cut off main branches early in the growth cycle.

If you want to walk under your tree, you must start in its early years to cut off all the low horizontal-growing scaffold branches so that, at maturity, it has no branches for 7 or 8 feet above

*A Red maple (*Acer rubrum*) shows care in pruning to develop shade for the home landscape.*

the ground. Branches that angle upward may be left at 5 or 6 feet up the trunk. The exception is a tree with drooping lower branches, such as the fruitless mulberry. In order to compensate for future drooping, you should cut off all branches at least 14 feet above ground.

Pruning mature trees

Perhaps when you bought your house there were established trees on the property. If these trees were kept in shape by periodic pruning, they don't need an initial heavy, corrective pruning. But if the trees were left to themselves and have developed into large, leafy problems, you will need to swing into action. Trees left unpruned may become too large for the space they were meant to occupy. They may also be lopsided, too close to the house windows or too dense for the good of the lawn and shrubs below. Overgrown trees first need thinning; then their overlong branches need heading back.

Thinning and heading neglected trees

The dramatic change that comes from transforming a lopsided or tangled tree into orderly symmetry should convince you that pruning is well worth the investment of time and energy required.

Crown thinning

Thinning the whole bulk or "crown" of the tree is an operation that benefits the whole tree. These are the main reasons for crown thinning:

(1) *To allow light to penetrate.* Removing some of the side branches allows light and air to penetrate the tree, contributing to its health. In addition, tree foliage may be blocking light from entering house windows or reaching plants below the tree.

(2) *To reduce resistance to the wind.* This is important to trees such as the evergreen elm that have a weak branch system. This elm grows so many leaves that its thin, fast-growing branches become vulnerable to wind damage.

(3) *To reduce the demands of heavy foliage on a fast-growing tree.* The tree may grow out of balance with its roots and eventually produce only poor quality, spindly new growth.

(4) *To reduce a tree's water needs.* The less foliage a tree has, the less water it will need to draw from the soil.

Crown reduction

Thinning will not reduce the overall size of the tree crown, only its density. To reduce the general size of a tree,

Ways to direct growth

For an open tree
Leave the terminal shoot on all scaffold branches and eliminate or shorten all laterals.

For a compact tree
Shorten all branches one-half, cutting to outward facing buds.

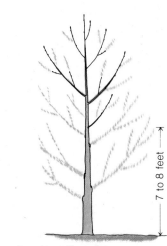

7 to 8 feet

For a tree to walk under
Cut off all branches 7 to 8 feet above the ground when the tree is tall enough to retain 3 to 4 scaffold branches. Branches that angle up may be left above 5 to 6 feet.

The Shapes of Trees

Trees come in all sizes and shapes. Their natural form is largely determined by the growing tip of the terminal shoot, pruning practices and environmental factors. By observing how the shoot tip of a young tree influences the buds below it, you should get some idea of the ultimate form or shape of the mature tree even though you had never seen the plant before.

On this page we have included eight of the more common shapes. And with each we have listed some of the more popularly planted species. There is always disagreement in such a subjective listing. Natural tree shapes are difficult to define on paper, but we'll make an attempt nevertheless.

Columnar

Sweet gum

Pyramidal arborvitae

Irish yew

Upright English oak

Incense cedar

American holly

Open Head Irregular

Sycamore

Scarlet oak

White oak

Valley oak

Hackberry

Sassafras

Ginkgo

Poplar

Weeping

Weeping willow

European white birch

Mayten tree

Australian willow

Weeping Higan cherry

Weeping mulberry

Broad Cone

Pin oak

Tulip tree

Little-leaf linden

English holly

Sorrel tree

Beech

Blue spruce

Douglas fir

Austrian pine

Globe

Norway maple

Sugar maple

Southern magnolia

Red horsechestnut

Ash

Tupelo

Chinese pistache

Catalpa

Fastigiate

Lombardy poplar

Italian cypress

Upright European hornbeam

Vase

American elm

Japanese zelkova

Pagoda tree

Crape myrtle

Autumn gold ginkgo

Serviceberry

Horizontal Spreading

Dogwood

Honey locust

Japanese maple

Red bud

Silk tree

Apple

Crabapple

Live oak

Goldenrain tree

you must head back the terminal branches. For a drastic reduction in size, you'll have to cut back to good lateral branches and even head back the tips of these. Since too drastic and quick a cutback will upset the balance between the roots and the crown, it's better to cut back in stages over several years.

Care should also be taken so you don't fall into the common practice of topping a tree and leaving the main leader topped or cut back to such a large diameter that it will never heal. This kind of topping leaves no branches above the open cut and invites decay to enter the main trunk of the tree. Future branches growing from such a decayed top can come crashing down during wind storms.

Water sprouts
As a general rule, cutting off one shoot near a healthy bud will produce two or more shoots. This is just another instance of nature's generosity to the good pruner. Sometimes, though, after long neglect, severe pruning will cause an outburst of many weak and spindly new shoots or a sudden appearance of thick, soft growths starting from dormant or adventitious buds.

Occasionally, one or two water sprouts can be left to fill a vacant space in the tree's structure. In this case, they are an unexpected bonus. But almost as many water sprouts may appear again the following year; if they do, they should be removed. If left, they will drain vigor from the main scaffold branches and spoil or delay your intended tree shape.

Eucalyptus
The eucalyptus creates a special pruning problem. In some of the larger varieties, whole branches may drop off unexpectedly for no apparent reason. These falling branches can harm people, plants and property.

Large branches of older eucalyptus trees can be stubbed back. Even if you saw off the whole crown of this tree or cut it off at ground level, its recuperative powers are so extraordinary that it will quickly grow another tree. You may have seen a eucalyptus whose head has been cut off so that it resembles a telephone pole, with no foliage left. A short time later, green shoots will emerge from the area of the cut and quickly grow into a full head of foliage.

Conifers
Conifers — pine, juniper, fir, spruce — are generally neglected by the average gardener, who will prune a maple on the right, an oak on the left, and skip the pine in the middle. By the time conifers reach the nursery, they have usually had several years of shaping, are symmetrically well-bal-

anced and already show the characteristic form of the variety. This leaves little for the home gardener to do.

As the years pass, you may suddenly realize that your pine has overgrown its allotted space. To remove an overgrown conifer and replace it with one that will stay smaller is an expensive waste. But you may have missed your chance to control the overgrown tree: heavy pruning may now be impossible because most conifers don't carry latent buds below the foliage area and do not readily produce adventitious buds. If a branch is cut back past the foliage area, the rest of that branch dies. Once lower branches are removed, they are gone forever; no new ones will take their place, except in the case of yews and some junipers.

Many people fear that conifers will bleed to death when pruned. This probably stems from ignoring the primary rule about pruning conifers; never prune more than one-third each year.

Conifers *can* be pruned, and a precise time of year is not important for most of them. However, if you want to keep conifers growing slowly and within the bounds of allotted garden space, prune them just after the new growth is completed, usually in late spring or early summer.

You can control the size and shape of random-branching conifers — arborvitae, sequoia and yew, for example — by shearing or tip pinching them. And you can form closer whorls in the whorl-branching species — fir, spruce and pine — if you head back new growth to a bud.

Pines pruned during a dry summer or in southern areas during any summer are prone to attack by bark beetles. Sometimes the beetles attack in such numbers that they will kill a tree.

Some conifers, if pruned while new growth is still soft, may develop new buds. If they are pruned after new growth has hardened, no new buds are formed and the pruned tips can become dead twigs.

Junipers, arborvitae, cypress and false cypress can be pruned safely at any time, but it is best to prune them before or during new growth, and avoid pruning in late summer.

After the plant is as large as you like, prune back all new growth except on conifers that are naturally large growing. You can shear the plants into formal shapes or, if you want a softer look and have the time, prune back branch tips individually with pruners or by hand pinching.

If you prune in the evening after watering the plant, using sharp shears, you'll avoid the needle burn (also called shear burn) that often occurs when a dry conifer is pruned.

Pruning conifers

Pine
Prune candles when small needles show. New buds for side growth break just behind where cut is made. Remove entire candle and growth of previous season's side branches will continue.

Juniper/Arborvitae
Prune when new growth is completed to slow growth. Heavier pruning should be done early so new growth can quickly cover any wounds.

Spruce
Prune new growth back half-way to promote density. Laterals should be cut back to a pair of buds or other laterals.

[For details on the pruning of other conifers like firs, hemlocks, redwoods and yews, see their specific entries in the pruning encyclopedia, pages 30 to 43.]

Radial and vertical spacing

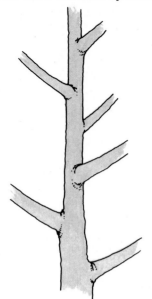

Major scaffold branches should be spaced vertically 18 to 24 inches apart (or more for larger trees). Five to seven main scaffolds should be evenly distributed radially. A perfect spiral is not necessary. The purpose is to prevent any one branch from growing directly over the other.

Water sprout pruning

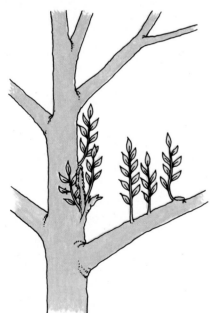

Water sprouts are the rapidly growing, thick soft shoots that appear after a tree suffers an abrupt, major change. They commonly appear after heavy pruning. They are not, however, strongly attached branches and rarely make good substitutes for the slower growing existing branches. Usually, water sprouts that do not fill a hole in the tree's framework are removed.

Cabling and bracing

These are mechanical methods for supporting weak crotches and branch systems of large trees. They are usually used for older trees with excessively heavy branches or decayed wood. Relatively difficult and expensive procedures, they can nevertheless prevent untimely damage and thereby significantly prolong the life of a tree that is beyond the help of simple pruning to reduce weight on a crotch.

Cabling is done high in the tree, ideally two-thirds of the distance from the crotch to the top. Heavy seven-stranded cable and forged-eye bolts are the preferred hardware. The goal of cabling is to link the branches of the crown so that they move as a single unit. Cables must be kept tight — loose they can do more harm than good.

Bracing is a rigid method of support. Heavy metal rod (specifically designed for this use) is threaded into the tree just above the weak crotch and must be bolted from both ends.

These procedures are best left to qualified arborists — consult with a company you trust. For more information, write: National Arborist Association, 3937 Stratford Road, Wantagh, New York 11793.

Pruning forest trees for profit

Before we get into advice on how to prune particular varieties of trees, we give general guidance to those readers who may have a woodlot and want to make a bit of cash from it.

Depending on the market, of course, money can grow on two types of trees — those that will end up as sawtimber or veneer and those that will be Christmas trees. The pruning methods for the two types are very different.

Sawtimber and veneer

The aim here is to minimize the number and size of knots in the tree trunk that will become a log. Live branches make tight knots and dead branches make loose knots, both of which degrade the quality and hence the price of the log.

The first major pruning of the tree should be done before its trunk reaches a DBH (diameter breast high or 4½ feet from the ground) of 4 to 6 inches. Usually the best tool for this job is the curved type of hand pruning saw that cuts only on the return stroke. Use it to remove all side branches from the trunk up to about 8 feet from the ground but *always* leave at least a third of the tree's total height in green crown. If you take away more of the crown, the tree's growth will slow down drastically.

As the tree continues to grow, the knots will remain in the core, which will eventually become 4x4 or 6x6 timbers, but the outer wood grows free of knots.

Always providing that at least a third of green crown is left intact, all limbs should be cut off before they reach 2 inches or more in diameter. With the many types of pine that put out a whorl of branches each year, no more than 3 vigorous green whorls should be removed at a time and no more major pruning should be done until three years later. Remember that pines need extra care to keep them safe from attack by bark beetles. Do not prune pines during a dry summer or during any summer in warm southern areas of the country.

Usually the second major pruning of timber trees should be done when all side limbs up to 17 feet above the ground can be removed while leaving at least a third of the green crown. The tree can then become a 16-foot sawlog or veneer log. Woodlot owners usually use a pole pruner for this job, but in commercial forests, a mechanical pruner is often used. It will climb the bole of a tree and remove all side limbs to a preset height above the ground.

It is often not economical to try to prune all the trees in your woodlot with a view to selling them as high-grade logs for lumber or veneer. Concentrate on the vigorously growing well-spaced trees and ignore the filler or trainer trees. They can be gradually removed and sold for pulpwood, small rough sawlogs or other low quality products.

Christmas trees

Some growers of Christmas trees aim at a fairly natural form in their trees, simply cutting off the ends of any branches that outgrow the others. But some growers prefer to keep their trees severely sheared in a tight conical form. These trees are usually very dense and ornaments cannot easily be hung except on the outer tips of the branches.

The best way and time to prune Christmas trees depend on the particular species. The information that follows on pruning ornamentals can be applied to pruning Christmas trees of those same species.

Two deservedly popular trees are shown in each of the four seasons: the taller Liriodendron tulipifera *(Tulip tree) and* Cornus florida *(Flowering dogwood).*

Alphabetical list of ornamental trees

This section is a digest of pruning information about commonly planted trees. It is not all-inclusive. The trees are listed alphabetically and cross-referenced under both their botanical and common names. If there is no widely used common name, the tree is listed only under its botanical name.

A tree may have many common names but it can have only one botanical name. For example, *Acer saccharum* is also known by the common names of Hard maple, Rock maple and Sugar maple. In the section that follows, all four of these names are listed but the information about the tree is found under the botanical name.

Three categories of information are given about each tree: *Characteristics*, which tell if a tree is deciduous or evergreen, and how it grows; *How to prune; When to prune.*

You should also know that the same pruning information will generally apply to a cultivar of the species from which it originated. As with all generalities, there are exceptions, and we've tried to point these out as they occur.

Abele
see Populus alba

Abies nordmanniana
(Fir, Caucasian fir, Nordmann fir)
Characteristics: Densely foliaged symmetrical conifer with strong central leader. Native to mountains of the West Caucasus. May grow to 200 feet but more commonly to 40 feet in cultivation.
How to prune: Pruning rarely necessary except to remove dead or broken branches. If bottom branches spread too wide, shear to contain. Avoid topping, which produces an unnatural, multiple trunked tree that needs constant attention. Also don't cut back into leafless wood or whole branch may die. If two leaders form when tree is young, remove the weaker. For a specimen tree (a tree that stands alone), it is recommended that you leave the bottom branches to the ground, and not prune it up to walk under.
When to prune: Before growth in spring is best but anytime will do.

Acacia baileyana
(Bailey acacia, Golden mimosa)
Characteristics: Wide-spreading (to 30 feet, and as high) single or multiple trunked evergreen. Profuse yellow flowers in early spring.
How to prune: Little pruning normally required. Narrow, V-shaped crotches that become weaker with age should be removed when young. For multiple trunks, head back leading growth thus encouraging lower branches. As single trunked tree, remove suckers that form around base. Mature specimens often become very dense — thin to open center of crown. Of course, dead wood should be removed.
When to prune: Anytime but after flowering will exert the greatest control over size.

Acacia melanoxylon
(Black acacia, Blackwood acacia)
Characteristics: Fast-growing evergreen that may reach 70 feet but more commonly reaches around 35 feet. Leaves (properly, "phyllodes") are feathery when young, becoming typically 4 inches long and 1 inch wide with age. Relatively short-lived but valued for tolerating poor growing conditions.
How to prune: Prune to shape when young to eliminate narrow crotches before they cause problems. May also be necessary to head back when young to promote wide spread. Prune to thin mature trees, eliminating dead wood.
When to prune: Summer is best but can be pruned anytime.

Acer species
(Maple)

Acer buergerianum
(Trident maple)
Characteristics: A low-spreading tree, often with multiple trunks, whose ultimate height rarely exeeds 30 feet. The shape of the leaf is the source of its common name: it has three sharp points.
How to prune: Remove lower branches to give room to walk under if desired. A strong tree, little pruning normally needed other than corrective — dead wood, crossing branches or branches growing too low.
When to prune: Dormant pruning is best though anytime is acceptable other than period of most active growth — springtime.

Acer negundo
(Ash-leaved maple, Box elder)
Characteristics: Fast-growing tree that may reach 50 feet, though usually less. Considered a "weed" tree where choice of maples is wide but useful in the arid southwest. Variegated leaf forms are preferred.
How to prune: Because of fairly brittle wood, early training should be directed to developing strong, widely angled and well spaced scaffold branches. When mature, thin crown to reduce wind resistance.
When to prune: When fully dormant is best.

Acer palmatum
(Japanese maple)
Characteristics: Small deciduous tree much admired for delicate texture. Slow in growing, may reach 30 feet high and 20 feet wide. Many cultivars available are even more restrained in growth. Can be easily maintained at any size.
How to prune: Handsome as either single or multitrunked. Best practice is simply to encourage natural habit: low-branching, ascending sharply with layered-looking twig structure. Little pruning required.
When to prune: When fully dormant is best; a twig or two during summer and fall won't hurt.

Acer platanoides
(Norway maple)
Characteristics: Deciduous, hardy tree that grows to 50 feet tall with a spread of 70 feet. A good shade tree often used for planting along streets. Many cultivars available of which 'Crimson King' is probably the best known.
How to prune: This is a stocky tree with heavy branches and a close crown. Small shoots arising from main branches should be left. Aside from removal of dead or crossing branches, little pruning is necessary. In areas of severe high winds, some thinning to open crown and reduce wind resistance is helpful.

When to prune: Almost all of the maples have a tendency to bleed when sap is rising in spring. Best to prune in late summer or when dormant.

Acer saccharinum
(River maple, Silver maple, Soft maple, White maple)

Characteristics: A deciduous tree growing fast to 40 feet, then slowly to 60 feet and more. Leaves are light green on top and silvery below. Gray to reddish tan bark has a handsome shaggy look. Care should be exercised when climbing into this tree. Its brittle branches can be extremely dangerous under one's weight. Also, large limbs breaking off during storms often cause a great deal of property damage. Some tree experts feel that *Acer rubrum* (Red maple, Scarlet maple) and its cultivars are far superior to *Acer saccharinum*. Prune *Acer rubrum* as for *Acer saccharum*, described in the next entry.
How to prune: Prune to correct natural faults of this tree: wood is relatively brittle and narrow V-crotches tend to form. Try to space scaffold branches widely along the central leader and choose ones with strong, widely angled crotches. Thin crown of mature trees to lessen wind resistance.
When to prune: Avoid pruning after growth starts in early spring — this is a profuse bleeder.

Acer saccharum
(Hard maple, Rock maple, Sugar maple)
Characteristics: One of the most common maples, particularly in the northeast, and probably the best. It's most visible when brightly colored in the fall. Maple sugar is derived from its sap and its wood is one of the best for furniture. It grows 80 to 100 feet tall and 60 to 80 feet wide.
How to prune: Maintain a single leader for 30 to 40 feet or as long as practical. Remove crossing secondary branches and watch for weak, tight crotches.
When to prune: Late summer or when dormant.

Aesculus x. carnea
(Buckeye, Red horsechestnut)

Characteristics: Deciduous tree that grows 30 to 50 feet high and nearly as wide. Pyramidal when young, mature tree develops a round crown. Spectacular reddish flower spikes 8 to 10 inches long in midspring.
How to prune: Doesn't require frequent pruning, just occasional attention to remove dead wood. Reduce interior branching of overly dense mature specimens.
When to prune: Winter or early spring before growth starts is best.

Albizia julibrissin
(Mimosa, Silk tree)
Characteristics: Grows fast to between 25 and 40 feet and spreads out even wider. Arching branches form umbrella like canopy. It is frequently multi-trunked.
How to prune: For typical umbrella form, establish first scaffold branches at about 8 feet from the ground, then top the tree when it reaches desired height. Wood is weak, so reducing weight on long horizontal branches is beneficial.
When to prune: Winter or early spring is generally best but wait until danger of frost is past in cold winter areas.

Alder
see *Alnus species*

Aleppo pine
see *Pinus halepensis*

Alnus species
(Alder)
Characteristics: Deciduous fast-growing trees. Moisture-loving roots may be invasive. Most develop straight trunks with a definite central leader, some branch from the base and may become large shrubs.
How to prune: If a single-trunked tree is desired, remove low-growing branches that compete. Small dead branches need annual removal.
When to prune: Anytime is alright but winter or early spring is usually easiest.

Amelanchier species
(Juneberry, Sarviceberry, Saskatoon, Serviceberry, Shadbush)
Characteristics: Lovely, small native tree with a range from Quebec to Georgia. Covered with flowers in early spring and

orange red leaves in fall. Usual height about 25 feet. Its edible fruits are like miniature apples.
How to prune: Most species tend to form many trunks. Choose the strongest one if single trunk desired. Often best, though, to allow natural form.
When to prune: Late winter or early spring before flowers show is best.

American arborvitae
see *Thuja occidentalis*

American elm
see *Ulmus americana*

American holly
see *Ilex opaca*

American sweet gum
see *Liquidambar styraciflua*

American yellowwood
see *Cladrastis lutea*

Arbutus menziesii
(Madrone)
Characteristics: An evergreen tree or large shrub native to a large area along the Pacific coast of North America. Most notable is its smooth reddish bark that is shed in thin flakes. Can reach 80 or more feet but around 30 feet is more common. Doesn't like to grow below an elevation of 300 to 400 feet above sea level.
How to prune: A very strong-growing tree when established, requiring only the removal of dead wood and interior branches to expose attractive bark.
When to prune: Early spring.

Ash-leaved maple
see *Acer negundo*

Aspen
see *Populus alba*

Acer platanoides
(Norway maple)

This young Norway maple was transplanted recently. After being staked for support, the top was severely pruned to compensate for root loss and to correct its poor structure. As the photographs show (taken over a period of six months), one main leader was chosen; all criss-crossing or too closely spaced branches were removed, and the tree was opened up. The result was a healthier tree, and the beginnings of an attractive mature form.

Atlas cedar
see Cedrus atlantica

Bailey acacia
see Acacia baileyana

Basswood
see Tilia cordata

Bay, Bay laurel
see Laurus nobilis

Bead tree
see Melia azedarach

Beech
see Fagus sylvatica

Beefwood
see Casuarina equisetifolia

Betula species
(Birch)

Betula nigra
(Black birch, Red birch, River birch)
Characteristics: Deciduous tree that grows rapidly when young, eventually reaching 65 to 70 feet. Shape is conical when young and becomes open and spreading.
How to prune: May divide at ground level and grow into large shrubs but best to prune to a single trunk. Remove branches attached with weak crotches and dead or diseased wood.
When to prune: Late summer or autumn. Cuts made in the spring tend to bleed profusely.

Betula pendula (also sold as *B. alba* and *B. verrucosa*)
(White birch, European white birch)
Characteristics: Weeping deciduous tree of lacy texture. Trunk and main branches develop white bark. Commonly 30 to 40 feet high and 15 feet wide.
How to prune: A slow healing tree that does not respond well to pruning. Take care to finish pruning cuts smooth and close to the trunk to enable the fastest possible callus formation. Necessary pruning includes removal of low-growing, dead or diseased branches.

When to prune: Best time is late summer or fall. Wounds made during growing season tend to bleed.

Birch
see Betula species

Black acacia
see Acacia melanoxylon

Black birch
see Betula nigra

Black gum
see Nyssa sylvatica

Black locust
see Robinia pseudoacacia

Black tupelo
see Nyssa sylvatica

Blackwood acacia
see Acacia melanoxylon

Blue gum
see Eucalyptus globulus

Box elder
see Acer negundo

Bradford pear
see Pyrus calleryana 'Bradford'

Buckeye
see Aesculus x. carnea

Bull bay
see Magnolia grandiflora

California bay
see Umbellularia californica

California incense cedar
see Calocedrus decurrens

California laurel
see Umbellularia californica

California live oak
see Quercus agrifolia

California pepper tree
see Schinus molle

Callery pear
see Pyrus calleryana

Calocedrus decurrens
(Incense cedar, California incense cedar)
Characteristics: Evergreen symmetrical tree grows to 70 feet, 30 feet wide at base. Native to wide area of western U.S. Pungent foliage in flat sprays.

How to prune: Most beautiful when left to assume natural form. You may want to remove the low branches. Never top. Can tolerate shearing and has been used as a hedge. For a specimen tree, you may want to leave lower branches to the ground.
When to prune: Anytime.

Camphor tree
see Cinnamomum camphora

Canoe cedar
see Thuja plicata

Carya illinoinensis
(Pecan)
Characteristics: Deciduous tree that may reach 100 feet but usually less. Spread is equal to height. Form is rounded crown.
How to prune: When young, space scaffold branches widely along the trunk. The mature tree needs little pruning. Simply remove the dead or diseased wood.

When to prune: Late summer, early spring or at greatest convenience.

Casuarina equisetifolia
(Beefwood, Horsetail tree)
Characteristics: Often mistaken for a pine but what looks like pine needles are actually jointed green branches, miniatures of familiar creekside horsetails *(Equisetum)*. Fifty feet high and half as wide. Most frequently planted as a seaside tree, especially in sandy soils. Also often used as a windscreen to protect citrus fruit trees.
How to prune: Generally not much pruning required. Young trees may try to develop several trunks — select the best and remove the others. Remove dead or broken branches annually. Generally not much pruning required.
When to prune: Anytime will do, spring is best.

Catalina ironwood
see Lyonothamnus floribundus asplenifolius

Catalpa species
(Indian bean)

Catalpa bignonioides
(Common catalpa, Southern catalpa)
Characteristics: Deciduous fast-growing tree to 40 feet, spreads nearly as wide. Large heart-shaped leaves and long (13 to 18 inch) pods.
How to prune: Train young tree to 12 feet before allowing extensive branching. Once branching begins, crown quickly opens. Left natural, branches will reach to the ground even on mature trees. Wood is weak so old trees may need their branches shortened to reduce weight. Tolerant of pollarding, especially when young.
When to prune: When dormant for major cuts, anytime for touch-up pruning.

Catalpa speciosa
(Catawba, Cigar tree, Northern catalpa, Western catalpa)
Characteristics: Similar to *C. bignonioides* but is larger and hardier, has larger leaves and fewer flowers. Fast-growing to 70 feet.
How to prune: Train tall, clear trunk when young. Branches originating 8 feet from the ground will eventually reach nearly to the ground.
When to prune: When dormant.

Catawba
see Catalpa speciosa

Caucasian fir
see Abies nordmanniana

Cedrus species
(Cedar)

Cedrus atlantica
(Atlas cedar)
Characteristics: Needled evergreen that grows 40 to 60 feet high and 30 to 40 feet wide. Broad-spreading crown when mature.
How to prune: Maintain central leader as long as practical — competing leaders tend to

split off, particularly if ice or snow laden. Remove dead wood as it appears as well as weak-growing branches lying against stronger ones. If desired, remove lowest growing branches to expose silver trunk.
When to prune: Before new growth in spring.

Cedrus deodara
(Deodar)
Characteristics: Needled evergreen, most refined and graceful of the cedars. Grows fast, 40 to 75 feet high and 20 to 35 feet wide. Nodding or hooked tip makes this tree easy to recognize at a distance.
How to prune: Maintain compact growth by cutting back new growth half way in late spring. Remove dead wood. Tolerates shearing.

When to prune: Late spring for greatest effect on size, or anytime.

Celtis australis
(European hackberry, Honeyberry, Lote tree, Mediterranean hackberry)
Characteristics: Deciduous, grows at moderate rate to about 50 feet and nearly as wide. Bears edible dark purple berries. Tough tree useful in arid western regions.
How to prune: Train major scaffold branches of young trees from about 8 feet off the ground. Watch for pendulous branches, weak crotches. Mature trees require little pruning.
When to prune: When dormant is best.

Cephalotaxus fortunei
(Chinese plum yew)
Characteristics: Evergreen conifer that resembles true yew *(Taxus)* but needles and fruits are larger. Can reach 30 feet but is often shorter.
How to prune: Usually produces two or three upright branches, with horizontal branches making a layered appearance. Little pruning required except to maintain shape as desired. New

growth will form from even the oldest growth.
When to prune: Best in springtime before new growth, or anytime.

Cercis canadensis
(Eastern redbud, Judas tree)
Characteristics: Fast-growing deciduous tree that flowers

profusely in early spring. Irregular round head may reach 35 feet high and as wide.
How to prune: May form multiple trunks unless otherwise trained. Little pruning required other than removal of dead wood. When mature, prune to maintain canopy shape. Minimum pruning avoids wounds and risk of disease.
When to prune: Late fall or early spring.

Chamaecyparis species
(False cypress)
Characteristics: A coniferous evergreen that grows in a narrow pyramid to 100 feet or more. Leaves are scalelike and arranged in sprays very similar to arborvitae *(Thuja* species). To distinguish them, turn the sprays upside down — *Chamaecyparis* has distinct white markings. Common species include *C. lawsoniana,* the Lawson cypress, a northwestern native that grows to 100 feet and is available in many forms. *C. nootkatensis,* the Nootka cypress, is an important timber crop of the northwest. It is somewhat more hardy than the Lawson cypress but should be protected from winter winds. *C. obtusa,* the Hinoki cypress, is an excellent ornamental but one of the least hardy. It is a favorite in its native Japan. Many cultivars are available. *C. pisifera,* the Sawara cypress, is also a native of Japan. It is taller growing (to 150 feet) and more open in habit (especially when mature) than the others. It is also one of the most hardy. Again, many cultivars are available. Generally, the species native to Japan are most used

in eastern North America.
How to prune: The Lawson cypress is an excellent hedge plant. Others require little beyond cleaning out of dead wood and debris that collects on the interior branches.
When to prune: Midspring is best but touch-up pruning in summer or winter is all right.

Chaste tree
see *Vitex lucens*

Cherry laurel
see *Prunus caroliniana*

Cherry plum
see *Prunus cerasifera*

Chinaberry
see *Melia azedarach*

China tree
see *Melia azedarach*

Chinese elm
see *Ulmus parvifolia*

Chinese pistachio
see *Pistacia chinensis*

Chinese plum yew
see *Cephalotaxus fortunei*

Chinese scholar tree
see *Sophora japonica*

Christmas holly
see *Ilex aquifolium*

Cigar tree
see *Catalpa speciosa*

Cinnamomum camphora
(Camphor tree)
Characteristics: Evergreen, grows slowly to 50 feet forming wide, round crown. Common street tree in many areas of the southwest. Also grown in the deep south. Yellow green leaves are aromatic, new leaves reddish.
How to prune: When young, direct scaffold branches to outside rather than up for most attractive mature form. When older, little pruning is necessary except to remove dead or damaged wood.
When to prune: Anytime is all right but major pruning in early spring allows full season for wounds to heal before winter.

Cladrastis lutea
(Virgilia, Yellowwood, American yellowwood)
Characteristics: Deciduous, with a moderate growth rate to 30 or 35 feet and spread about 20 feet. Growth is upright and form eventually vase-shaped. Fragrant, white, pealike flowers hang in clusters in June. Good against drought, heat and cold; and in alkaline and wet soils.
How to prune: Wood is somewhat brittle. Young trees need to be pruned to keep leader growing as long as possible and to avoid weak crotches. Do this by shortening side branches as they appear. This helps the tree achieve its best shape and distributes the weight of a mature crown.
When to prune: Will bleed from pruning wounds in spring. Best to wait until late summer or while dormant.

Coast redwood
see *Sequoia sempervirens*

Colorado spruce
see *Picea pungens*

Common blue gum
see *Eucalyptus globulus*

Common catalpa
see *Catalpa bignonioides*

Cornus florida
(Dogwood, Flowering dogwood)
Characteristics: Beautiful de-

ciduous tree native over a wide area of eastern U.S. May reach 30 feet high and as wide. Flowers in early spring.
How to prune: Most beautiful if left unpruned. Don't remove low branches, particularly in cold areas, as these shade bark from sun after freezing nights.
When to prune: When dormant is best.

Cottonwood
see *Populus alba*

Crabapple
see *Malus floribunda*

Crape myrtle
see *Lagerstroemia indica*

Crataegus laevigata
(Hawthorn, English hawthorn, White thorn)

This three-year-old Crataegus is being pruned to give it good structural shape. All suckers and water sprouts were pruned off, its twigginess and criss-crossing branches were eliminated, and weak branches with narrow branch angles were removed. This will enable the tree to grow strong and healthy but a watchful eye should be kept on the tree throughout its life. If fire blight disease is a problem, remove the infected twigs well below the dead wood, and remember to disinfect your pruning shears afterward.

Crataegus laevigata
(Hawthorn, English hawthorn, White thorn)

Characteristics: Deciduous, moderately fast-growing tree that reaches 20 feet high and about 15 feet wide. The toughest of the flowering trees. Flowers may be white, pink, or red, single or double. Some varieties are fruitless. They're thorny and make a tough hedge.
How to prune: Little pruning required but may develop many water sprouts that should be removed in June. Dense crown that usually develops may require thinning to reduce wind resistance. Fire blight disease can be a problem — remove infected twigs well below dead wood and remember to disinfect pruning shears afterward.

Tolerates shearing to become useful as hedge.
When to prune: When dormant.

Cupressus arizonica
(closely related to C. *glabra*, smooth-barked Arizona cypress)
(Arizona cypress, Rough-barked Arizona cypress)
Characteristics: A 40-foot evergreen, may reach 70 feet at the most. It grows narrow and pyramidal when young but eventually develops a broad and open crown. The state tree of Arizona, it is valuable for shade and shelter throughout the southwest. Greatest weakness is shallow roots that may allow wind-toppling. Sometimes available grafted onto more hardy roots.
How to prune: It is often pruned heavily. However, cypress wood is slow to recover from pruning wounds and heavy cutting seems to predispose the tree to other problems. Otherwise, allow development of a single central leader and remove dead, broken or diseased branches.
When to prune: Spring or early summer is best.

Cupressus macrocarpa
(Monterey cypress)

Native to the central California coastline, it thrives where constantly buffeted by sea winds. Height may reach 65 feet but is usually less. It grows in apparently impossible conditions of soil and exposure. A tree of great character, it usually suffers in cultivation.
How to prune: Some shear it as a hedge but that practice is not advocated. It is best left to natural form. Yellowing leaves turning dark red indicate a fungus disease for which the only cure is to remove the tree.
When to prune: Spring, early summer if at all. Winter pruning has been fatal.

Cupressus sempervirens
(Italian cypress)

Characteristics: Narrow, strongly fastigiate varieties are most common. Most will grow to 50 or 60 feet and stay less than 15 feet wide. Do not water or fertilize too much or excessive horizontal growth will develop. Dead twigs are usually the result of girdling by twig borers.
How to prune: Little is normally required. To manicure, shear yearly and wrap with twine.
When to prune: Spring or early summer is best.

Deodar
see *Cedrus deodara*

Dogwood
see *Cornus florida*

Douglas fir
see *Pseudotsuga menziesii*

Eastern redbud
see *Cercis canadensis*

Eastern white pine
see *Pinus strobus*

Elaeagnus angustifolia
(Russian olive)
Characteristics: A tough deciduous that is great in hot dry areas. Its only requirement is well-drained soil. The leaves are willowlike, olive green on top and silvery beneath. Growth rate is fast, particularly when young. Branches are thorny; bark is dark brown and sheds; Fragrant yellowish flowers in early summer followed by small, olivelike fruits.
How to prune: Usually a very self-sufficient tree. Encourage a strong central leader and wide-angled scaffolds when young. Branches may become too long and prone to break so some tip pruning will be beneficial. Old wood contains many dormant buds that will sprout after severe pruning. Frequently used as hedge plants and will tolerate shearing.
When to prune: Midsummer is the best time.

Elm
see *Ulmus species*

English hawthorn
see *Crataegus laerigata*

English holly
see *Ilex aquifolium*

Eucalyptus ficifolia
(Flaming gum, Red-flowering gum, Scarlet-flowering gum)
Characteristics: An intermediate-sized eucalyptus forming a round head about 25 feet high and as wide. Notable for its bright red flowers. Thrives in coastal areas. Frost tender.
How to prune: Tends to be low branching so head back low branches to promote a higher crown, taller single trunk. Remove suckers and dead or broken branches. Prune off

large seed pods after flowering.
When to prune: Spring is best.

Eucalyptus globulus
(Blue gum, Common blue gum)
Characteristics: This is the giant eucalyptus that was widely

planted throughout California during the 1800s. Still popular as a windbreak. Bark is shaggy and leaves are about 7 inches long and sickle-shaped. A good tree in its place but don't use it where a 100-foot (and higher) tree would be too tall.
How to prune: Not a garden plant — requires constant pruning to contain its growth. Thinning to reduce weight on branches may be necessary

but on a tree this size, pruning is usually a job for professionals. Remove suckers and dead wood. It can recover from severe topping.
When to prune: Eucalypti tolerate pruning anytime but spring is best.

European beech
see Fagus sylvatica

European hackberry
see Celtis australis

European larch
see Larix decidua

European mountain ash
see Sorbus aucuparia

European white birch
see Betula pendula

Evergreen Chinese elm
see Ulmus parvifolia

Evergreen pear
see Pyrus kawakamii

Fagus sylvatica
(Beech, European beech)
Characteristics: Deciduous, slow-growing to 70 or 80 feet with a spread of 60 feet. Dense pyramidal form. These are trees prized for their smooth gray bark and glossy dark green foliage.
How to prune: Select just one leader if the tree does not do this naturally. Multiple leaders are a common cause of limb splitting in older trees. Beeches naturally grow in groves, and planted in groups 40 or 50 feet apart, they are more likely to grow up straight and tall. As

they become older, remove lowest branches to reveal the handsome trunk.
When to prune: When dormant is best.

False acacia
see Robinia pseudoacacia

False cypress
see Chamaecyparis species

Fir
For true fir, see Abies nordmanniana; for Douglas fir, see Pseudotsuga menziesii

Flaming gum
see Eucalyptus ficifolia

Flowering dogwood
see Cornus florida

Flowering plum
see Prunus cerasifera

Fraxinus pennsylvanica
(Green ash, Red ash)
Characteristics: Deciduous, grows medium fast, typically to

45 feet, with a broad oval crown. Many cultivars are available, such as 'Marshall Seedless' and these have a more pyramidal form. A favorite lawn tree casting a light shade.
How to prune: Requires some training when young to grow to its best form. Head back low side branches to promote growth of central leader. Select wide angled branches as main scaffolds. As dense crown develops, lower branches often die back from lack of light — remove them as needed.
When to prune: Fall or when dormant are best times to prune.

Giant arborvitae
see Thuja plicata

Giant cedar
see Thuja plicata

Giant redwood
see Sequoiadendron giganteum

Giant sequoia
see Sequoiadendron giganteum

Ginkgo biloba
(Ginkgo, Maidenhair tree)
Characteristics: Deciduous tree that can reach 60 or even 100 feet. Growth rate varies with climate. Conical and sparsely branched when young, becoming more dense and spreading with age. Fall color brilliant yellow. Leaves usually all drop at once. Only male forms should be planted.
How to prune: This tree usually forms a strong central leader but if secondary leads develop, remove them. Multiple leaders are a common cause of weak-

ness in mature specimens. Of course, remove dead and diseased wood as necessary. Old trees are self-sufficient, requiring little extra care. With grafted male forms, remove rootstock suckers.
When to prune: Early spring is best.

Gleditsia triacanthos inermis
(Honey locust, Thornless honey locust, Honeyshuck)
Characteristics: Deciduous fast-growing trees native over a large part of eastern and central U.S. The wild tree has thorns that can be up to 4 or more inches long, especially on the trunk. Now cultivars of the thornless variety are planted exclusively. 'Sunburst' grows to about 40 feet and 'Shademaster' to about 60 feet.
How to prune: The vigor of these improved varieties may result in quite long new growth on twigs and branches of young

trees. If this happens, remove about one-half of the new growth in midsummer. Older trees of reduced vigor benefit from severe pruning every two to four years.
When to prune: Late fall or early winter is best.

Golden-chain tree
see Laburnum watereri 'Vossii.'

Golden mimosa
see Acacia baileyana

Golden-rain tree
see Koelreuteria paniculata

Grecian laurel
see Laurus nobilis

Green ash
see Fraxinus pennsylvanica

Grevillea robusta
(Silk oak)
Characteristics: Fast-growing evergreen to 50 or 60 feet and sometimes higher. Spread is 20 to 35 feet. Pyramid-shaped when young but becomes round topped. Fernlike leaves are dark

green on top and silvery below. Tolerates drought and compacted soil.
How to prune: Wood is brittle and breaks easily in high winds. Develop strong branching system by selecting wide angled scaffolds. Heading back at planting time can strengthen the tree. Prune lightly each year to avoid production of suckers. Can be sheared for use as tall hedge.
When to prune: Best after flowering in early summer.

Gum tree
see Eucalyptus species

Hard maple
see Acer saccharum

Hawthorn
see Crataegus laevigata

Hemlock, Hemlock spruce
see Tsuga species

Hickory
see Carya illinoinensis

Holly
see Ilex species

Honeyberry
see Celtis australis

Honey locust
see Gleditsia triacanthos inermis

Honeyshuck
see Gleditsia triacanthos inermis

Horsetail tree
see Casuarina equisetifolia

Ilex species
(Holly)

Ilex aquifolium
(Christmas holly, English holly)
Characteristics: Slow-growing evergreen to 60 feet although average height is around 40 feet. Grown primarily in the Pacific Northwest. Numerous cultivars are available, all with lustrous foliage and most with bright red fruit.
How to prune: These very adaptable plants tolerate many kinds of pruning treatments, including shearing. To train as

a tree, select a single leader when young. Then head back vigorous branches as necessary to maintain shape. Fruits are borne on previous year's wood.

When to prune: Around Christmas is convenient as clippings are useful for indoor decorations. Pruning any time of year is all right.

Ilex opaca
(American holly)
Characteristics: A pyramid-shaped evergreen tree common in the eastern U.S. May reach 50 feet high. Usual color of berry is red but on some cultivars is orange or yellow.
How to prune: When young, promote the dominance of a single leader and shear for pyramidal habit. Later, head individual branches as necessary to maintain shape. For specimen tree, allow the branches to grow to the ground. However, if you want to feature the bark or the trunk, remove the lower branches. The American holly can withstand heavy pruning. It should be heavily pruned when transplanted. Fruits are borne on current year's wood.
When to prune: Like the English holly, it can be lightly pruned almost any time of year. However, it should be kept in mind that heavy pruning after it flowers or during the summer could stop the holly from forming berries.

Incense cedar
see Calocedrus decurrens

Indian bean
see Catalpa species

Indian lilac
see Melia azedarach

Jacaranda acutifolia
(Jacaranda)
Characteristics: Deciduous native of Brazil grows fast to 30 feet high and 25 feet wide. Open, irregular head and often multitrunked. One of the most beloved trees of southern Cali-

fornia. Blue flowers usually from May to July.
How to prune: Needs extra training when young to develop best form. Select one trunk if several are competing. Single-trunked form is much stronger. Mature trees need only occasional heading back.
When to prune: Before spring growth.

Japanese flowering crabapple
see Malus floribunda

Japanese maple
see Acer palmatum

Japanese pagoda tree
see Sophora japonica

Japanese zelkova
see Zelkova serrata

Judas tree
see Cercis canadensis

Juneberry
see Amelanchier species

Koelreuteria paniculata
(Golden-rain tree, Varnish tree)
Characteristics: Deciduous, grows moderately fast to 25 or 35 feet. Rounded outline, wide-spreading branches give a flat look to the top. Covered with yellow flowers by late spring. Flowers in July in the northeast, Ohio and in the mountains of North Carolina. Drought tolerant and pest free.
How to prune: Very little pruning is required. Select strong scaffold branches when training the young tree. Remove

dead, diseased or ill-placed wood of an older specimen.
When to prune: Winter pruning is best.

Laburnum watereri 'Vossii'
(Golden-chain tree, Vossii laburnum)
Characteristics: Deciduous, grows moderately fast to 20 or 30 feet, forming a dense, upright, vase-shaped crown. Ordinary looking when not in bloom but is spectacular when loaded with 18-inch, tapering clusters of rich yellow flow-

ers. Does not do well in hot climates.
How to prune: To train as a tree rub off buds along bottom of trunk. Severe pruning may rejuvenate an older tree. Prune annually to keep neat. Avoid large pruning wounds because they heal slowly.
When to prune: After flowering or as late as August. In early spring, wounds bleed excessively.

Lacebark elm
see Ulmus parvifolia

Lacebark pine
see Pinus bungeana

Lagerstroemia indica
(Crape myrtle)
Characteristics: Deciduous that grows slowly to between 10 and 30 feet. Form is vase-shaped. Best to train to a single stem. A favorite tree because

of its late summer profusion of showy flowers and colorful mottled bark.
How to prune: Prune for desired shape and also to favor flowering. Remove suckers, branches, dead or diseased wood. Flowers are borne on the current season's growth, thus a heavy pruning when dormant to stimulate growth of new wood in spring will promote the heaviest flowering.
When to prune: When dormant, although touch-up pruning can be done anytime.

Larix decidua
(European larch)
Characteristics: Unusual because it's one of the few deciduous conifers. Growth habit is a slender pyramid, widening with age, to 50 feet high. Beautiful in spring when new leaves appear and in fall when they become yellow orange. It grows medium-fast, is widely adapted.
How to prune: Encourage central leader, although tree often grows with a good straight trunk naturally. Suppress bottom branches if necessary. Do not top unless unavoidable, for

topping will destroy this tree's beauty.
When to prune: Anytime is all right. Pinch branch tips in spring or early summer to limit spread and keep dense.

Laurel
see Laurus nobilis

Laurus nobilis
(Bay, Bay laurel, Grecian laurel, Sweet laurel)
Characteristics: Compact evergreen with multiple trunks that grows slowly to 20 feet in a compact, almost conical form. A well-behaved tree, the source of the bay leaves used in cooking.
How to prune: A shapable tree that can adapt to even the severe pruning of topiary. Lower branches naturally grow close to the ground. If pruned up to expose the trunk, expect prolific suckering.
When to prune: Spring or summer pruning is best for controlling speed and shape of growth.

Linden
see Tilia cordata

Liquidambar styraciflua
(Sweet gum, American sweet gum, Red gum)
Characteristics: Deciduous, grows moderately fast to 90 feet. Symmetrical when young, with a strong central leader spreading and forming a more rounded crown with maturity. Maplelike leaves, prickly fruits the size of golf balls are identifying characteristics. Good fall color.
How to prune: Little training is required. When young, space scaffolds widely along trunk to establish strong framework. It naturally forms branches close to ground; preserve these if at all possible.
When to prune: When dormant.

Liriodendron tulipifera
(Tulip tree, Tulip poplar, Yellow poplar)
Characteristics: Fast-growing deciduous tree native to east-

ern U.S. Tall pyramidal form reaches as high as 150 feet, though usually half that in cultivation. Appreciated for its uniquely shaped bright green leaves that create a beautiful light canopy.

How to prune: Though wood is somewhat brittle, generally a strong tree that requires little pruning. Most important is to train with strong central leader. Remove upright shoots that arise from major laterals.

When to prune: Wintertime, dormant pruning is best.

Littleleaf linden
see *Tilia cordata*

Live oak
see *Quercus virginiana*

London plane
see *Platanus acerifolia*

Lote tree
see *Celtis australis*

Lyonothamnus floribundus asplenifolius
(Catalina ironwood)
Characteristics: A small evergreen tree native to Santa Cruz Island off the coast of southern California. Leaves fernlike but leathery. Flowers white, fragrant and profuse. Ultimate height usually about 25 feet, spread about 15 feet.

How to prune: Remove dead flower clusters. Can tolerate severe pruning and can be kept as a hedge. Impressive as a low-branched single specimen. Prune to single trunk when young to train as a tree. Will readily "stump-sprout" if cut off at base.

When to prune: In winter for greatest growth control. Can also be pruned in summer.

Madrone
see *Arbutus menziesii*

Magnolia grandiflora
(Bull bay, Southern magnolia)
Characteristics: One of the world's finest flowering trees. Native to the southern U.S. but most of the cultivars originated and are grown and used in the west. A broad leaf evergreen that may reach 80 feet in height, it bears fragrant creamy white flowers that measure 8 inches or more across.

How to prune: Usually requires little attention. Prune when young to establish main framework. Remove interior water sprouts as they form. For better flowering, thin lightly in early spring.

When to prune: Anytime will do but early spring is best.

Maidenhair tree
see *Ginkgo biloba*

Malus floribunda
(Crabapple, Japanese flowering crabapple)
Characteristics: One of the most widely adapted of all the flowering trees. Over 600 species and varieties are grown in North America. Deciduous tree that flowers heavily in spring in colors ranging between white and red. Normally has rounded

crown with arching branches. Good in lawns and rows. Provides edible fruit in the fall. Average size fruit of this flowering crabapple is about ⅜-inch in diameter: birds love them.

How to prune: Train when young with the modified central leader method (see apple trees in Chapter 5) and continue this method if pruning for fruit. Annual pruning to thin is beneficial. Less frequent heavier pruning may overstimulate and produce too much unwanted growth.

When to prune: Branches removed before flowering in spring can be forced indoors. Otherwise anytime after flowering is fine.

Maple
see *Acer species*

Maytenus boaria
(Mayten)
Characteristics: An evergreen native of Chile, grows slowly to about 40 feet with a 20-foot spread. Small leaves on long

hanging branches lend a graceful look. Tolerates heat, soil salinity and coastal conditions.

How to prune: Train to either single or multiple trunk as desired. This is a tree that tends to suckers — remove them, of course. Periodic thinning of crown and trimming of low hanging branches may be necessary.

When to prune: Spring or fall pruning is best.

Mediterranean hackberry
see *Celtis australis*

Melia azedarach
(Bead tree, Chinaberry, China tree, Paradise tree, Persian lilac, Texas umbrella tree, Umbrella tree)
Characteristics: Deciduous, grows to 35 feet high and as wide. Most common is the variety 'Umbraculifera.' Purple flowers are followed by *poisonous* yellow berries. Good shade tree in desert areas.

How to prune: Little pruning needed other than infrequent removal of dead wood and crossing branches.

When to prune: Responds best to pruning in fall.

Mimosa
see *Albizia julibrissin*

Mock orange
see *Prunus caroliniana*

Monterey pine
see *Pinus radiata*

Morus alba
(White mulberry)
Characteristics: Fast-growing deciduous tree with wide spread, reaches about 35 feet in height.

Fruitless varieties are most desirable. Lives no more than 20 years or so unless well cared for. Good temporary tree but is brittle and splits easily. Takes desert heat.

How to prune: Prune when young to aid development of strongest structure. In first three to five years cut back

Lagerstroemia indica
(Crape myrtle)

Crape myrtles are beautiful summer flowering small trees or shrubs. To maintain its size and to increase flower production, pruning is required annually, during the dormant season. This shrub was pruned back to about two feet, and the heavy pruning created a pollarded effect. Older dead wood was removed at the base, and all suckers were removed. The result was a lower, less dense shrub which will produce an abundance of flowers on new wood in the summer.

Pinus bungeana
(Lacebark pine)

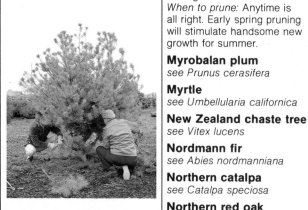

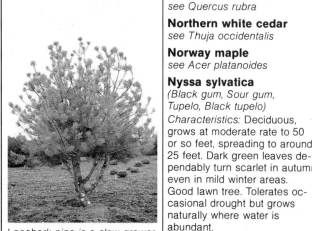

Lacebark pine is a slow grower and looks much like a large evergreen shrub. One of the most noted characteristics is its gray bark which flakes off to give it a lacey appearance. To accentuate this, lower branches can be removed, thus exposing the attractive bark and giving the plant a multi-trunk tree appearance.

new growth 20 to 30 percent at outward-upward facing shoots or buds. Develop 3 to 5 scaffolds with 3 to 5 arms. More tends to weaken the tree. Severe "dehorning" or stubbing back of branches will shorten its life.
When to prune: When dormant is best.

Myoporum laetum 'Carsonii'
Characteristics: Large broadleaf evergreen shrub or (with training) small tree. Grows fast. Excellent as seashore windbreak. Roots may be invasive.
How to prune: If allowed to grow into natural form, requires little attention. If pruned to form single or multitrunked tree, thin crown annually to reduce wind resistance and top heaviness. Can be rejuvenated by severe cutting back.
When to prune: Anytime is all right. Early spring pruning will stimulate handsome new growth for summer.

Myrobalan plum
see Prunus cerasifera

Myrtle
see Umbellularia californica

New Zealand chaste tree
see Vitex lucens

Nordmann fir
see Abies nordmanniana

Northern catalpa
see Catalpa speciosa

Northern red oak
see Quercus rubra

Northern white cedar
see Thuja occidentalis

Norway maple
see Acer platanoides

Nyssa sylvatica
(Black gum, Sour gum, Tupelo, Black tupelo)
Characteristics: Deciduous, grows at moderate rate to 50 or so feet, spreading to around 25 feet. Dark green leaves dependably turn scarlet in autumn, even in mild winter areas. Good lawn tree. Tolerates occasional drought but grows naturally where water is abundant.
How to prune: As the tree becomes established, remove lower branches. This will accommodate the pendulous habit of the tree and also allow clearance for walking under. If a low crown is desired, top the tree no taller than 20 feet.
When to prune: Fall or when dormant.

Oak
see Quercus species

Olea europaea
(Olive tree)
Characteristics: Evergreen native of Mediterranean and

western Asia. Grows fast in youth, then slows, eventually reaching 20 to 30 feet. Trunk is gray and commonly gnarled. Leaves are gray green with silvery undersides. If intended for ornamental use only, fruitless varieties such as 'Swan Hill' are preferred. In specimen size, one of the most reliable to transplant.
How to prune: Tolerates heavy pruning. Therefore, you can make it a tree, shrub or hedge. To train as tree, shorten side branches below where you want main scaffold branches to begin. To develop multiple trunks, simply select strong looking suckers and train them along desired direction. Fewer than five trunks is desirable. Excessive pruning often produces excessive and unattractive growth, so it is best to thin a little each year.
When to prune: Pruning after flowering will decrease olive production. Pruning after harvest will save the olive crop. Thinning can be done anytime without damaging the tree.

Olive tree
see Olea europaea

Oregon myrtle
see Umbellularia californica

Oregon pine
see Pseudotsuga menziesii

Oxydendrum arboreum
(Sourwood)
Characteristics: A deciduous native of eastern U.S., grows slowly to 35 or more feet with a pyramidal form. One of the most attractive small flowering trees. Large pendulous sprays of white flowers borne in June-July. Fall color is a brilliant scarlet. Requires acid soil. There is no competition from lawn or other plants.
How to prune: Relatively little required. When young, maintain a central leader and remove narrow-crotched branches early. Allow branching close to ground as this helps develop strongest trunk.

When to prune: When dormant or during the fall.

Paradise tree
see Melia azedarach

Pecan
see Carya illinoinensis

Pepperwood
see Umbellularia californica

Persian lilac
see Melia azedarach

Picea abies
(Norway spruce. Prune as for Picea pungens in next entry)

Picea pungens
(Colorado spruce)
Characteristics: Evergreen conifer, grows symmetrically 80 to 100 feet but garden specimens are rarely over 50 feet. Several cultivars are available, many with bluish leaves. Know the spruce by rolling needles between fingers — they are squarish in cross-section; when removed, the needles leave a peg or twig. The cones hang.

How to prune: Besides removal of an occasional dead branch, little pruning required. To stimulate denser growth, cut new growth back about half-way. If leader is lost at a young age, select and train a new one. Lowest branches can be removed if necessary for clearance but best if left alone.
When to prune: Just after new growth in spring to reduce growth rate, or anytime.

Pine
see Pinus species

Pin oak
see Quercus palustris

Pinus species
(Pine)

Pinus bungeana
(Lacebark pine)
Characteristics: Slow-growing to 75 feet. Common name comes from habit of scaling off bark similar to sycamore. Holds needles five years or longer. They are 3 to a bundle, 3 inches long. A very desirable

ornamental pine.

How to prune: Frequently grows with several picturesque trunks. Wood tends to be weak. Because bark is interesting, prune to show it to best advantage. As with all pines, never cut back past a twig or visible bud as the branch will probably die.

When to prune: Anytime will do but after new growth will help develop most compact and dense growth.

Pinus halepensis
(Aleppo pine)
Characteristics: Relatively slow to start but then grows quickly to 50 feet. Form is open and round-topped with short branches. Sparse foliage and spindly when mature. Needles usually in pairs and 2 to 4 inches long.

How to prune: Best to let this tree follow its own inclinations. As with other pines, cutting back candles before needles show will stimulate more compact dense growth. Never leave a branch stub without needles.

When to prune: Just after new growth, but removing the occasional dead wood can be done anytime.

Pinus radiata
(Monterey pine)
Characteristics: Very fast-growing to between 60 and 100 feet.

Native to coastal California. Pyramidal when young, becoming roundish with age. Needles in trios usually but sometimes pairs; bright green and 4 to 6 inches long. Lopsided, 7-inch cones may persist many years. Good tree for coastal windbreak, large hedge or screen.

How to prune: Tolerates enough pruning to be useful as a hedge but actually requires little. To control size, cut back candles before needles show. Cutting them back two-thirds will slow growth more than cutting back one-third. Pines have few "adventitious" buds — ones ready

to grow but invisible — so never leave branch stub expecting new branches to sprout.

When to prune: Most pruning of pines is best done after new growth and candle elongation in spring. Some pruning can be done anytime without harm.

Pinus strobus
(White pine, Eastern white pine, Soft pine, Weymouth pine)
Characteristics: A fast-growing tree from the Appalachian Mountains to north Georgia. May grow to 150 feet and live to over 450 years. Widely planted in the northeast. Many cultivars are available. Needles are 5 to a bundle and between 3 and 5 inches long.

How to prune: As with the other pines, little pruning is required. If desirable, the growth of this pine can be slowed somewhat by shearing when young to pyramidal shape. Guidelines given above for the other pines are also true for this one.

When to prune: After new growth in spring.

Pistacia chinensis
(Chinese pistachio)
Characteristics: Deciduous native of China, grows at moderate rate to 50 feet and nearly as wide. Spreading, umbrella-like crown. Widely adapted but prefers abundance of summer heat. An excellent lawn or street tree, one of the best for providing a filtered shade. Good yellow fall color in mild climates. Dioecious.

How to prune: When young, train to a single leader, selecting well-spaced scaffolds. Then prune to force lateral growth of these scaffolds. When mature, periodically thin ill-placed limbs, remove dead wood, and especially reduce weight on scaffolds.

When to prune: When dormant — branch structure is more apparent and pruning is therefore easier.

Platanus acerifolia
(London plane, Sycamore)
Characteristics: Fast-growing deciduous tree develops spreading crown at 40 to 60 feet. One of the best for cities as it is tolerant of poor growing conditions and smog. Attractive green and white flaking bark. No fall color but has brown ball-shaped fruits borne in clusters of two. Highly subject to leaf anthracnose disease, causing premature leafdrop in the spring and twig dieback in severe cases.

How to prune: When young, select primary scaffolds at the height necessary for expected traffic underneath: 6 to 10 feet

would be typical. After that, little is required but to remove occasional dead branches. Will tolerate pollarding but this is a high maintenance type of training that is rarely justifiable.

When to prune: Fall or winter when dormant is best.

Poplar
see *Populus alba*

Populus alba
(Abele, Aspen, Cottonwood, Silver-leaved poplar, White poplar)
Characteristics: Fast-growing deciduous tree. Wide-spreading and about 50 feet high when mature. Leaves shaped like small maple leaves are dark green above and silvery white underneath, very attractive fluttering on a breezy day. Particularly useful at the seashore as it is tolerant of salt spray.

How to prune: Train when young to develop central leader and widely spaced scaffolds. When mature, remove dead or broken wood. This tree is most notable for prolific root suckers that, unless removed, will grow into full trees.

When to prune: When dormant before January because pruning wounds will bleed if sap is rising.

Portugal laurel
see *Prunus lusitanica*

Prunus caroliniana
(Cherry laurel, Mock orange)
Characteristics: Evergreen shrub easily trained to a small

tree, a native from North Carolina to Texas. As a tree, may reach 40 feet with trunk a foot thick. Best along coast but tolerates dry heat and wind. White flowers; small black fruit is highly favored by birds.

How to prune: Trained as a tree, it needs pruning only to shape. When young, select widely angled scaffolds. Can also be sheared or even used for topiary.

When to prune: After new growth in spring and again in the fall to maintain a formal shape. When convenient if growing naturally.

Prunus cerasifera
(Cherry plum, Flowering plum, Myrobalan plum)
Characteristics: Deciduous, grows to 30 feet high and often as wide. Bears small, red to yellow plums annually which are edible. Flowers are white and about an inch wide. Cultivars are available.

How to prune: When young, prune to establish strong framework — choose a central leader with widely spaced scaffolds to 10 feet or so, then top the leader. Also, prune to remove poorly placed limbs and water sprouts.

When to prune: Most should be done when dormant. Twigs removed when buds show color can be forced indoors. Pinching after flowering helps control shape.

Prunus lusitanica
(Portugal laurel)
Characteristics: Evergreen native of Spain, Portugal and the Canary Islands. Beautiful when allowed to develop naturally, usually with multiple trunks. Small white flowers in 10-inch clusters in spring. Fruit is red at first, becoming dark purple. Relatively tolerant of heat, sun and wind. Good

background plant.

How to prune: If left natural, little pruning is required. But with frequent clipping or even shearing, formal shapes are easily maintained.

When to prune: Anytime will do if growing naturally. Late spring is best for pruning to formal shapes.

Pseudotsuga menziesii

(Douglas fir, Oregon pine)

Characteristics: Evergreen conifer native from Alaska through British Columbia and western U.S. into Mexico. Fast-growing for the area, sometimes reaching 200 feet although usually less. Typical spread is 50 feet. A premier timber tree outproducing many other species. Stiff branches droop on lower part of tree, extend upward and outward on upper part. Soft, flat, bluish green needles arranged spirally on twig. New spring growth is an attractive apple green. Fragrant and fresh smelling. Unlike true firs, cones hang and cone scales have 3-pronged bract.

How to prune: Train to central leader and replace it if natural one is lost. Pinch new growth on horizontal limbs to make growth more compact and reduce weight on branches. Topping will cause the immediate decline of an older tree but those trained from youth can be sheared and used as a hedge.

When to prune: After new growth in spring to slow growth.

Pyrus callervana 'Bradford'

(Bradford pear, Callery pear)

Characteristics: Deciduous, grows at a moderate rate to oval-shaped tree 50 feet high and about 30 feet wide. The 'Bradford' cultivar is superior: thornless, resistant to fire blight, with smaller fruits, abundant white bloom in early spring, brilliant crimson red in fall. Other cultivars are available.

All are adaptable to stresses of growing in a city or on the coast.

How to prune: Does not demand frequent pruning. When young, train to central leader with strong scaffolds. Later, prune to remove criss-crossing limbs and dead wood, or to maintain shape. Remove basal rootstock suckers.

When to prune: Fall and when dormant.

Pyrus kawakamii

(Evergreen pear)

Characteristics: Evergreen spreading shrub easily trained to tree form. Grows at moderate rate to 30 feet with open, irregular crown. Year-round attractiveness of shiny, light green, wavy-edged leaves is major virtue. White flowers from late winter to early spring.

How to prune: Adapts to several training methods — espalier, shrub and tree — but the natural multiple-trunked form is quite beautiful, especially if laterals are thinned to expose trunks. To train as a tree, select just one trunk and laterals at the desired heights. Pinching back these laterals to buds facing upwards and outwards will tend to strengthen them. If removing wood infected with fire blight, cut well into apparently healthy wood (12 inches or so) and disinfect shears afterward.

When to prune: Prune in spring to induce greater flowering, or anytime.

Quercus species

(Oak)

Quercus agrifolia

(California live oak)

Characteristics: Evergreen leaves like holly with tufts of minute, white hairs near center of undersides. Native of the California coastal mountain ranges. Once far more prevalent, so remaining specimens should be preserved. Handsome wide-spreading tree

when mature that may reach 70 feet and over 100 feet wide. Bark is fairly smooth and light gray.

When to prune: When young, pinching back unnecessary twigs will speed growth. Until well-established, prevent formation of multiple leaders and branches too close to the ground. Select wide angled scaffolds (most are that way naturally) 10 to 12 feet from the ground. Mature specimens need pruning only to remove dead wood, crossing branches or out-of-place limbs.

When to prune: Anytime is all right, but major pruning should be done in summer so as not to overstimulate spring growth, which is mildew-susceptible.

Quercus coccinea

(Scarlet oak)

Characteristics: Deciduous native of eastern U.S. named for brilliant fall color. Grows moderately fast with open-branching habit to 70 feet. Has the familiar oak leaf, deeply cut with pointed lobes. Is especially subject to borer injury. Excellent lawn tree.

How to prune: Train when young to central leader with well-spaced scaffolds. With maturity, only occasional corrective pruning is required.

When to prune: When dormant.

Quercus palustris

(Pin oak, Spanish oak)

Characteristics: Deciduous eastern U.S. native grows rapidly to 60 or 70 feet. The easiest oak to transplant successfully, best in acid soils. Leaves are glossy, dark green and deeply cut, with pointed lobes. Branches stay low to the ground until fully mature. Good lawn tree.

How to prune: Relative to other oaks, requires more help when young. Watch to insure development of central leader and choose rather high scaffolds as they tend to droop considerably. This characteristic should be watched if it might cause a

problem, as with street trees that might interfere with traffic. However, if you remove the lower branches, the next higher set often begins to droop.

When to prune: When dormant.

Quercus rubra

(Red oak, Northern red oak)

Characteristics: Fall color almost as spectacular as *Q. coccinea.* Deciduous and fast-growing. Can reach 90 feet high. Typically deep cut leaves with pointed lobes, they're reddish when new and deep red in the fall. A high branching, deep-rooted tree.

How to prune: A very self-sufficient tree but give it some attention at first to insure best placement of scaffolds. Mature specimens need only rare removal of dead wood or crossing branches.

When to prune: When dormant.

Quercus virginiana

(Live oak, Southern live oak)

Characteristics: Sturdily branched, wide-spreading oak that is usually evergreen but becomes partly deciduous at the northern limit of its range. A spectacularly branched tree, it reaches 60 feet in height and an enormous 100 feet or more in width. Leaves are smooth-edged, whitish below and shiny on top.

How to prune: A massive oak of particularly strong limbs. Frequently branches very close to

ground. Allow to follow natural habit and do only corrective pruning.

When to prune: As necessary.

Quickbeam

see Sorbus aucuparia

Red ash

see Fraxinus pennsylvanica

Red birch

see Betula nigra

Red-flowering gum

see Eucalyptus ficifolia

Red gum

see Liquidambar styraciflua

Red horsechestnut
see Aesculus carnea

Red oak
see Quercus rubra

Redwood
see Sequoia and Sequoia-dendron

River birch
see Betula nigra

River maple
see Acer saccharinum

Robinia pseudoacacia
(False acacia, Black locust, Yellow locust)
Characteristics: Deciduous native of east central U.S. Fast-growing to between 40 and 75 high by 30 to 60 feet wide. An attractive tree in many ways but faulted for its heavy thorns, invasive roots. Good for tough situations — heat, drought, poor soil and neglect — but borers can cause problems.
How to prune: With care, first of all, because of the 3-inch thorns. Maintain central leader to 30 feet if possible because multiple leaders weaken the tree. Select strong, wide-angled scaffolds widely spaced. Remove broken wood frequently. Self-propagates rapidly — remove the young unless you want a grove.
When to prune: Bleeding can be a problem, so mid to late summer is best time.

Rock maple
see Acer saccharum

Rowan
see Sorbus aucuparia

Russian olive
see Elaeagnus angustifolia

Salix babylonica
(Weeping willow)
Characteristics: Moisture-loving, fast-growing deciduous tree that matures at about 45 feet high, spreading somewhat wider. Appreciated for graceful drape of greenish yellow branchlets nearly to ground. Probably most attractive and best used at stream or lakeside. Tends to be short-lived.
How to prune: Train to single stem for 15 feet. Keep pinching branches lower than this to direct energy to the main stem. Remove dead wood as necessary.
When to prune: Fall is best but anytime will do.

Sarviceberry
see Amelanchier species

Saskatoon
see Amelanchier species

Sassafras albidum
(Sassafras)

Characteristics: Deciduous native of eastern woodlands. Variably shaped leaves of none, two or three lobes. They'll remind you of mittens. Excellent fall color. May be difficult to transplant.

How to prune: Train to single stem for as long as possible. As the tree matures, remove branches to about a 7-foot height to reveal deeply furrowed bark. Root suckers if damaged — remove the suckers unless you want a colony (or remove carefully and use to propagate). Prune as necessary when mature.
When to prune: Fall or when dormant.

Saw-leaf zelkova
see Zelkova serrata

Scarlet-flowering gum
see Eucalyptus ficifolia

Scarlet oak
see Quercus coccinea

Schinus molle
(California pepper tree)
Characteristics: A misnomered evergreen, it's native to Peru, Bolivia and Chile. Has a long history of usefulness in California, however, and is well adapted to poor soils, drought and wind. Texture is fine and habit is weeping, making a most pleasing silhouette. Faults include invasive roots that often win over sidewalks and curbs.
How to prune: Since it will grow into a large shrub if ignored, prune a young tree high, maintaining a single stem if you want a tree to walk under. Resist making cuts larger than 4 inches if possible — it will bleed at any time of year and is highly susceptible to wood-decaying fungus diseases. Frequent light thinning of the crown is best. Can even be maintained as 4-foot hedge if kept constantly clipped.
When to prune: Spring is best for any major or extensive work, anytime for touch up.

Serviceberry
see Amelanchier species

Sequoia sempervirens
(Redwood, Coast redwood)
Characteristics: Evergreen conifer naturally adapted throughout the California and Oregon fog belt, where it receives moisture all year round. One of the world's tallest — to 350 feet — and most magnificent trees. In the garden, it is fast-growing to 60 feet. Form is a narrow pyramid. Most attractive in small groves, and cultivars are now available.
How to prune: Only corrective pruning is necessary, though you may want to remove sucker growth from the burl. Can be used as a hedge if planted close and annually topped and trimmed.
When to prune: As necessary. To maintain formal shape, after spring growth is best.

Sequoiadendron giganteum
(Giant redwood, Giant sequoia)
Characteristics: Evergreen conifer native to the west slope of the Sierra Nevada mountain range in the western U.S. A massive tree that holds limbs 100 feet off the ground as big as the biggest elm. One is 37 feet in diameter at its base and estimated to be 3,000 years old. Foliage is a dull green. A distinct pyramidal habit when young, branching to the ground. Requires less water than the coast redwood.
How to prune: Can be trimmed to pyramidal form when young to stimulate most compact growth, otherwise only infrequent removal of dead wood

is needed. Always remove branches to main trunk.
When to prune: As necessary.

Shadbush
see Amelanchier species

Shinglewood
see Thuja plicata

Silk oak
see Grevillea robusta

Prunus lusitanica
(Portugal laurel)

The Portugal laurel is a useful screen plant because of its dense, dark evergreen foliage. This overgrown hedge is being sheared not only to keep it within bounds, but also to make it more dense. Pruning was done in late spring. It may need attention again in the fall.

Tilia cordata
(Basswood, Linden, Littleleaf linden, Small-leaved European linden)

Tilia is a deciduous, slow to moderate growing tree with a strong pyramidal shape. When young (as it is shown here) it should be pruned to shape. This tree had many basal and lower branches which needed to be removed to allow for under canopy traffic or an under planting. Select scaffolds that are widely spaced. As this young tree gets older it will only need corrective pruning.

Silk tree
see Albizia julibrissin

Silver-leaved poplar
see Populus alba

Silver maple
see Acer saccharinum

Small-leaved European linden
see Tilia cordata

Soft maple
see Acer saccharinum

Soft pine
see Pinus strobus

Sophora japonica
(Chinese scholar tree, Japanese pagoda tree)
Characteristics: Deciduous native of Japan and Korea, grows fairly slowly to 60 or 75 feet, with an equal spread. Dense and upright when young, becoming round and spreading. Large clusters of wisteria-like flowers appear late summer. Compound leaves like ferns become attractive clear yellow before falling. Pods remain throughout winter. A tough tree that tolerates city conditions. It is also a good substitute in

shape and habit for the troubled American elm.
How to prune: When young, maintain the central leader as long as possible and select strong scaffolds. Periodically remove weight on lower branches by thinning.
When to prune: Late summer — wounds made in spring may bleed profusely.

Sorbus aucuparia
(European mountain ash, Quickbeam, Rowan)
Characteristics: Deciduous native of Europe and Asia grows at moderate rate to 25 feet. Narrow when young, becomes rounded with maturity. Favored for large clusters of bright orange-red berries that appear late summer and early fall.
How to prune: The tree is

prone to somewhat narrow and weak crotches, so thin these while it is young to avoid the considerable work that will be required as the tree ages. Leave lower branches on the trunk but constantly pinch them so they don't compete with the leader. Maintain the leader to

10 feet, selecting strongly connected, wide angled scaffolds.
When to prune: Fall or when dormant.

Sour gum
see Nyssa sylvatica

Sourwood
see Oxydendrum arboreum

Southern catalpa
see Catalpa bignonioides

Southern live oak
see Quercus virginiana

Southern magnolia
see Magnolia grandiflora

Spanish oak
see Quercus palustris

Sugar maple
see Acer saccharum

Sweet gum
see Liquidambar styraciflua

Sweet laurel
see Laurus nobilis

Sycamore
see Platanus acerifolia

Taxus species
(Yew)
Characteristics: Dense-growing, needle-leaved evergreens. Many cultivars of varying forms are available. The two most widely used species are T. baccata, the English yew, and T. cuspidata, the Japanese yew. Both species grow very slowly, ultimately reaching 50 or 60 feet, and live a long time. The Japanese yew is more tolerant of cold so is the more frequent choice in areas where winters are cold.
How to prune: Among the most widely used topiary and hedge plants, yews grow so slowly that formal, neat shapes are

retained with only annual shearing (see Chapter 11). If the natural tree shape is desired, encourage development of the central leader. Prune the young tree two or three times a year until desired height is reached.
When to prune: Anytime will do but late winter is best time for heavy pruning.

Texas umbrella tree
see Melia azedarach

Thornless honey locust
see Gleditsia triacanthos inermis

Thuja occidentalis
(American arborvitae, White cedar, Northern white cedar)
Characteristics: Coniferous evergreen native to southeastern Canada. Grows fairly slowly to 45 feet with a narrow pyramidal form. Leaves are like scales and arranged on sprays that tend to turn upward at the tips. Good hedge or tall screen.
How to prune: Requires only touch-up trimming if growing naturally. Often used as hedges (see T. plicata below for pruning).
When to prune: Before new growth in spring so cuts are concealed quickly. A light pruning after growth will help maintain shape.

Thuja plicata
(Canoe cedar, Giant arborvitae, Giant cedar, Shinglewood, Western red cedar)
Characteristics: Widespread throughout western U.S. where it grows slowly to between 130 and 200 feet. Bright to dark green lacy foliage on slender branches. Most handsome in large open areas when lowest branches allowed to sweep the ground. Also good hedge or screen plant.
How to prune: This is an even more successful hedging plant than T. orientalis. Allow to grow about a foot higher than hedge height desired, then top the leader back 6 inches below desired height and trim laterals at the desired height. This method will make a good top surface. If you're not using for hedge, little pruning is required.
When to prune: Prune to conform to shape before new spring growth. Touch up in late spring or early summer to hold shape longer.

Tilia cordata
(Basswood, Linden, Littleleaf linden, Small-leaved European linden)
Characteristics: A pyramid-shaped tree that reaches 30 to 50 feet with a spread of about half that. Flowers are fragrant and are used by man to make perfume and by bees to make

an excellent honey. Tolerates adverse conditions of cities. Good lawn, street and shade tree. Many improved cultivars are available.
How to prune: When young, train to provide best structure. Direct growth toward leader and select widely spaced scaffolds. Occasional corrective pruning necessary when mature; can be trimmed as a hedge.
When to prune: Fall or when dormant.

Trident maple
see Acer buergeranum

Tsuga species
(Hemlock, Hemlock spruce)
Characteristics: Among the most delicate and graceful needle-leaved evergreens. Needles are about ¾-inch long, somewhat flattened, and have 2 silvery-white bands lengthwise on the bottom side. When they fall, a small protruding peg is left where the needle was attached. The Canada hemlock *(T. canadensis)* is a native of northeastern North America. It is hardy and grows to about 80 feet. The western hemlock *(T. heterophylla)* grows naturally along the northwestern coast from Alaska to California. It favors the moist, coastal regions and may grow to 200 feet high. Both species develop into outstanding specimens, especially in lawns.
How to prune: Very little pruning is required if grown naturally. However, if the leader is lost, replace it by training a nearby branch upward. Most remarkable about the hemlocks is their tolerance of heavy shearing. For this reason, they are frequently used as hedge plants and can be kept sheared at manageable heights.
How to prune: Midsummer is best. Young, fast-growing hedges may require an additional early spring clipping.

Tulip poplar
see Liriodendron tulipifera

Tulip tree
see Liriodendron tulipifera

Tupelo
see Nyssa sylvatica

Ulmus americana
(American elm, White elm)
Characteristics: Probably the most widely planted American native tree. Beautifully vase-shaped, fast growing to 120 feet. Leaves have sawtooth margin and are divided unevenly by the center vein, giving a lopsided look. The future of the species is now threatened by the Dutch elm disease, but much work is being done to protect the remaining specimens, and to discover forms resistant to the disease.
How to prune: Pruning tolerated but needed infrequently. Remove and destroy diseased wood, broken or rubbing branches. Bark beetles that carry the Dutch elm disease breed in the dying and broken branches.
When to prune: Fall or when dormant for major work but touch up anytime.

Ulmus parvifolia
(Chinese elm,
Evergreen Chinese elm,
Lacebark elm)
Characteristics: Usually partly evergreen but may lose leaves in zero temperatures. Fast growing medium-sized tree that forms an oval crown. Most notable is its peeling bark that makes the trunk rusty brown dappled with pale yellow. Good for reestablishing a tree canopy in new residential areas.

How to prune: Train young tree to single leader that begins branching at about 12 feet. Thin overcrowded crown in winter to reduce wind resistance. Frequent thinning is preferred because occasional drastic pruning promotes flush of unattractive growth.
When to prune: Fall or winter.

Umbellularia californica
(California bay, California

laurel, Myrtle, Oregon myrtle, Pepperwood)*
Characteristics: Evergreen native of the Pacific Coast. Grows slowly to 70 feet and frequently as wide. Much smaller under cultivation. Leaves glossy on top, dull green below and aromatic when crushed — can be used as a seasoning substitute for the common bay leaf. Small yellow flowers in spring followed by green, inedible fruits (considered "inedible" by some although American

Indians roasted and ate them) that gradually turn black. Wood valued for sculpting.
How to prune: Mature tree rarely needs pruning other than to remove dead or diseased wood. Thin to reduce shade if desired. In the garden, train to a single leader.
When to prune: Early spring or fall.

Umbrella-tree
see Melia azedarach

Varnish tree
see Koelreuteria paniculata

Virgilia
see Cladrastis lutea

Vitex lucens
(Chaste tree, New Zealand chaste tree)
Characteristics: Evergreen, slow to moderate grower to 50 feet. Form is round and spreading. Compound leaves of 5 ruffled 3-inch leaflets of rich, lustrous green. Small, pink, bell-shaped flowers followed by rose red, inedible fruits of cherry size. Requires better than average soil — a choice specimen for a choice location.
How to prune: Train young tree to central leader with well-spaced scaffolds beginning around 10 feet. When mature, prune when necessary to remove damaged or out-of-place limbs.
When to prune: Fall or when dormant.

Vossii laburnum
see Laburnum watereri 'Vossii'

Weeping willow
see Salix babylonica

Western catalpa
see Catalpa speciosa

Western red cedar
see Thuja plicata

Weymouth pine
see Pinus strobus

White birch
see Betula pendula

White cedar
see Thuja occidentalis

White mulberry
see Morus alba

White pine
see Pinus strobus

White poplar
see Populus alba

White thorn
see Crataegus laevigata

Yellow locust
see Robinia pseudoacacia

Yellow poplar
see Liriodendron tulipifera

Yellowwood
see Cladrastis lutea

Yew
see Taxus species

Zelkova serrata
(Japanese zelkova, Saw-leaf zelkova)
Characteristics: Deciduous native of Japan and Korea that is closely related to and commonly used as a substitute for the American elm. Grows fast to between 50 and 60 feet with an equal spread. Bark gray, leaves an attractive russet in fall. Good lawn or street tree. Improved selections are available.
How to prune: Maintain leader to at least 7 feet. Choose strong, widely spaced scaffolds.
When to prune: Fall or when dormant.

Fruit and Nut Trees

How do you prune for good quality fruit? Here's one place where you can compare apples with oranges, not to mention apricots, avocados, cherries, figs, grapefruit, lemons, peaches, plums, quinces, walnuts and pecans.

Pruning for good quality fruit

No other plants in the garden are so dependent on pruning as fruit trees. Unfortunately, no other group varies so widely in the ways of pruning. So if you want to grow beautiful crops of apples or peaches, then you must learn the differences between pruning an apple and a peach tree.

During the first three years of cultivation, most fruit and nut trees are pruned in much the same ways for basic form. When they begin to bear fruit, however, each species should be pruned differently. All bearing fruit trees can be pruned every year, with additional light pruning in the summer to expose fruit spurs. Nut trees usually need pruning only every other year.

Commercial fruit growers prune fruit trees in several ways. Each has advantages. A few orchardists use the older method called "vase pruning." An alternative and more popular method is called "modified central-leader pruning." A third way, "delayed open-center pruning," combines both methods. Remember that dwarf trees require less severe pruning since their ultimate height is less.

Vase pruning

The tree is shaped to a short trunk of about 3 feet with 3 or 4 main limbs, each of which has fully filled out secondary branches. This shape offers the advantage of an open center; light can penetrate to all branches. Vase pruning is always used with apricots, plums and peaches — and often with pears, apples and olives.

Modified central-leader pruning

The tree is shaped to one tall trunk

Part of an abandoned orchard being reclaimed, this fig has just been lightly pruned. Eventually all dead wood should be cut away.

that extends upward through the tree, clearly emerging at the top. This shape makes a strong tree but since the center is shaded, less fruit is produced. The smallest dwarf apples are pruned in this shape in a variation called the "spindle bush." Since the tree is as small as a bush, shade and pruning are no problem.

Delayed open-center pruning

This method produces both the strength of a central trunk and the sunny center of a vase-shaped tree. A single trunk is allowed to grow vertically until it reaches 6 to 10 feet; then it is cut off just above a branch. Main scaffold branches are then selected and pruned to form a vase shape. Subsequent prunings follow the vase method.

Pruning citrus

Pruning young fruit trees

When you plant a young bare root tree, it will usually consist of only a thin vertical shoot called a whip, and some twiggy side branches. Head the whip back after planting to balance the loss of roots that were cut away when the tree was uprooted.

You'll want to know how to prune fruit trees so they will grow to produce good quality, not just a quantity of fruit. A good fruit-producing tree should be low enough so that you can reach the fruit easily, strong enough to support itself and open enough for sun and air to penetrate. The branches should radiate around the trunk almost equally apart and emerge from the trunk at as close to a right angle as possible.

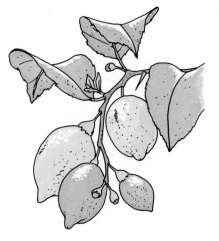

Pinch

Cut

Generally, don't worry about thinning citrus fruits unless a branch is about to break. Lemons, for example, tend to grow at the tips of thin branches. This overloads and may break them.

To correct this tendency, cut all laterals in half and pinch back new growth several times during the summer.

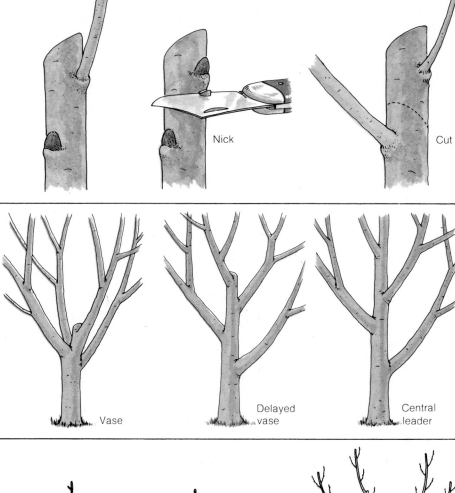

The new apple tree

You can start the vase method with apple trees as follows: After heading back, the bud immediately below the cut always emerges at too narrow an angle and will eventually develop into a new central leader. A scaffold branch trained from a narrow-angled bud will be weak. To correct this problem, nick the stem just below the bud. Nutrients will be diverted to the bud below, which will grow at a wider, stronger angle. The following dormant season, cut the weakened top bud off.

Nick

Cut

Fruit tree training methods

Vase: The center is open to allow light and air to penetrate and this encourages fruit on the lower branches.

Delayed vase: This is a compromise between the vase and central leader methods. It combines the strength of the central leader with the sunny center of a vase shape.

Central leader: This method results in a strong tree that can hold a crop well and stand up to rough weather.

Vase

Delayed vase

Central leader

Vase method pruning for three seasons

This is the training method we recommend for most fruit trees. Prune fairly heavily when the tree is young to establish the framework. Then prune as lightly as possible. Apples and pears usually require the least pruning to maturity, apricots and plums a little more, and peaches the most. When mature, most pruning is simply to maintain the established form.

First dormant season

Second dormant season

Third dormant season

Walnut tree training

Laterals that develop on new scaffold branches usually grow out at undesirably narrow angles. Remove such laterals and select new ones from buds the following year. They will produce wider-angled, stronger crotches.

First season bud forms a narrow, weak crotch

Remove

Secondary bud forms a wider angled, stronger crotch

The purpose of continuing to prune a mature tree is to keep the tree balanced in form and — very important — balanced in new and young wood. Left unpruned, the tree would become dense with weak twiggy growth; overloaded with small unhealthy fruit; or stop bearing altogether.

If you want a productive fruit tree, it's necessary to establish a definite method of pruning from the time the tree is planted.

Training the vase pruning way

When you plant a bare root fruit tree, cut off the central stem or whip (it is as yet too thin to be called a trunk) about 2 to 3 feet above the ground. The shorter length is for a dwarf, the longer for a standard tree. Cut just above a bud. Prune any side branches back to 2 buds.

First dormant season

After the new tree has grown through the first spring, summer and fall into its first winter dormancy, choose 3 or 4 branches with wide crotches. Look for branches that radiate evenly around the trunk by examining the tree from above and select 3 branches with almost equal distance between them. You should also try to have at least 6 inches vertical distance between branches; the lowest branch should be about 18 inches above the ground. If there are 3 such branches, cut the vertical stem off just above the top selected branch. If there are fewer than 3 good branches, leave the vertical stem and choose the remaining scaffold branches during the next dormant season.

Second dormant season

If still necessary, choose remaining scaffold branches and cut off the vertical stem just above the top selected scaffold branch. The scaffold branches you chose during the first dormant season will have grown side branches. Cut off the weakest of these, leaving the main stem and laterals on each branch. *But do not prune twiggy growth.*

Third dormant season

Now is the time to thin surplus shoots and branches. Select the strongest and best-placed terminal shoot near the tip of each scaffold branch, as well as 1 or 2 other side shoots on each branch. Then remove all other shoots on the branch. Leave the short weak shoots that grow straight from the trunk to shade it and help produce food for the tree.

A good rule of thumb for when to thin the five fruits depicted at the right is when the fruit has gone through half its growing season. How much? For apricots, 2 to 3 inches between fruits; plums, 3 to 4 inches; nectarines, 4 to 5 inches; peaches, 5 to 6 inches; and apples, 8 inches.

Thinning fruit

Apricots

Plums

Nectarines

Peaches

Apples

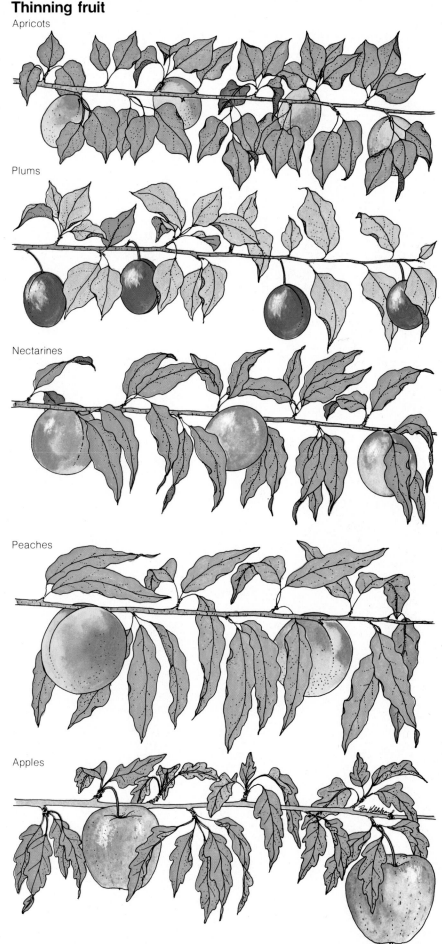

Pruning the fruitbearing tree

After the third season in the ground, a fruit tree will need only light thinning until it begins to bear fruit. Specific instructions on how to prune each kind of fruit tree appear in the following sections. Here we make just a few main points:

About a month before the fruit is to be picked, *summer pruning* can be done to expose the fruit to more light and air. Shorten new shoots to 3 or 4 inches wherever this will bring sunlight to the fruit on the branch.

It is always necessary to *thin the fruit* if you want large size, top quality fruit for home use. Otherwise nature will have her way in producing the most fruit in order to get the largest number of seeds to perpetuate the species. Cherries are the only exception and are rarely thinned at all.

Although each variety has its best time for thinning, a good rule of thumb is to thin before the fruit has gone through half of its growing season. In other words, you thin an early variety much earlier in the summer than the later maturing sorts.

Apricots should be thinned to about 2 to 4 inches between fruit; and peaches, nectarines and the larger plums to about 4 or 5 inches. For the top size of apple, leave about 6 to 8 inches of space and no more than one apple per fruit spur. The tree has only so much food and energy, and you have the choice of one large apple or two or more small ones.

If you would like to see how much difference thinning can make, leave a branch unthinned and observe its fruits at harvest time.

Left: The 'Fuyu' persimmon can be eaten when the flesh is still firm like an apple's. Other persimmons, however, must be fully ripened before eating. All require little or no pruning. Establish strong scaffolds when young, but control size by cutting each year to strong laterals. Thinning is unnecessary.

Apple trees

There are several sizes — heights at maturity — of apple tree that may be planted in the home garden.

The "standard" apple is a large tree, the standard for the commercial apple industry in this country. Usually the tree will reach 25 to 35 feet at maturity, depending on the variety and the way it has been pruned. This size is really too big for most home gardens.

The "semi-dwarf" is the next size down. In most varieties it will reach a height of about 15 to 18 feet, a satisfactory size for many gardens. It produces more fruit per tree than the true dwarf. Like the true dwarf, it begins to bear apples sooner than the standard tree. It should be emphasized here that the apples produced on the standard, semi-dwarf or dwarf tree will be the same size on each tree

of the same variety. The size of the fruit does not depend on the size of the tree.

The true "dwarf" or smallest of all apple trees was bred for garden growing only. It is 8 to 10 feet high at maturity. This is ideal for most home gardens and lets you have more than one apple tree even in a smallish garden. In fact, if your space is very limited, you can try planting two or three dwarf apples of different varieties in the same hole and treat them as one multitrunked tree.

Pruning standard apple trees

Vase pruning has been the common method used by commercial orchardists in training standard trees. The bare root tree is cut off to about 30 or 36 inches above the ground when planted. The scaffold branches will grow out from the trunk the first year and should be selected the following dormant season. Pick 3 or 4 branches evenly spaced around the trunk of the tree and at different

heights from the ground. Cut one-third of the length from these scaffold branches to encourage a strong branch system near the trunk that will hold your future crop of fruit. Cut away the other scaffold branches.

In the second and third dormant season, reduce the length of all new growth by one-third and thin out to create a strong, evenly spaced framework of branches. These secondary scaffold branches are the ones that will develop fruit spurs on their laterals. The pruning during this period should always be to a bud on the top of a branch that points outwards. This will cause the typical vase shape to develop.

The modified central-leader system is not recommended for a standard tree.

Pruning semi-dwarf and dwarf apple trees

While open head or vase pruning can be used with the smaller trees, other systems give better results faster. However, if you decide you like the vase-shaped tree, head the dwarf or semi-dwarf back to 2 feet when the bare root tree is planted and then trim exactly as for a standard tree.

The modified central-leader system seems to make semi-dwarfs and dwarfs earlier bearing and stronger. And, since the trees are small anyway, you won't have any trouble picking the fruit from the top of the tree.

Cut all branches, including the top, back about one-fourth or about 8 to 10 inches when planting the bare root dwarf. These cuts should be made to a strong outside bud. The second and third year, repeat the process to train the central leader up and the scaffold branches out parallel to the ground. Most dwarfs will begin to bear the second and third years and bear heavily thereafter.

Apricot trees

The apricot tree produces fruit on the previous season's shoots but the bulk of the fruit

appears on 4-year-old spurs on older wood and the spurs drop soon after. To encourage these spurs, pinch the lateral shoots when they are about 3 inches long.

Heavy pruning is essential to encourage the apricot to keep producing. Otherwise, it will start fruiting with heavy crops but the crops will dwindle as lush foliage shades the lower fruit spurs. Fruit will then be borne only high in the tree.

Plan to shape the young apricot to a wide-spreading head and keep it low. To maintain this shape, a tree will have to be severely thinned and headed yearly. A good apricot tree has a stubby look and no long, thin branches. The rule is to remove a third of the new wood each year by both thinning and heading. Do this in the winter when the tree is dormant.

When the fruit spurs on a branch are three years old — you can tell by counting the annual bud scar rings — select a new lateral branch and remove the old one the fourth season. The fruit will then appear mainly on the new branch; first, on last season's shoots and, in subsequent seasons, on spurs growing on that branch. Remove a third of the older lateral branches each year.

Avocado trees

Many of us have grown avocado seeds for interesting house plants. However, we must handle them differently if we expect to pick avocados in our back yard. There are some varieties that will stand temperatures down to about 20°F (-6°C) but the avocado is a truly southern tree that will take only very little frost.

It is best to buy your tree from a nurseryman who has budded or grafted a selected

Apple trees

This apple tree (variety 'Mutsu') has not been pruned for 2 years. Neglect has resulted in smaller sized apples which were borne high in the tree making harvest difficult.

In order to get the tree to produce larger, more accessible fruit, the top branches were reduced in height and some of the center branches removed to allow more light into the center of the tree.

variety onto a hardy understock and can tell you what to expect. Avocados are monoecious, and plantings should include several cultivars chosen for their pollen value.

The tree tends to grow somewhat upright, so early pruning is needed to keep the fruit in sunlight and within reach. If your new tree is not branched, cut the terminal growth off to about 30 inches of the stem and develop the scaffold branches by the modified central-leader system, much as you would a semi-dwarf apple tree (see above). A few varieties will bush out naturally and others will grow upright and require more heading. Mature avocados will require little pruning other than to trim out badly spaced, weak branches and to keep the center open.

Sweet cherry trees
Bare root trees should be cut back to about 30 or 36 inches from the ground. As the sweet cherry grows it should be pruned to the modified central-leader system, already described. Make sure that the leader or upper scaffold branches are not choked by lower scaffold branches that grow upwards. After the tree begins to bear, prune only weak branches out or those that develop at odd angles or cross another branch. Be sure to head back the leader and upright side branches to no more than 12 to 15 feet so that the mature tree can be kept at about 20 feet.

Sour cherry trees
The tree that gives you pie cherries differs from the sweet cherry tree in that it tends to spread wider and is considerably smaller. In fact, some varieties are almost like large bushes. The sour cherry can be pruned as a modified central-leader or, if you prefer to

keep the tree smaller, the vase shape can be used. It is quite easy to keep the sour cherry under 12 feet with either system.

Citrus trees
Oranges, lemons, grapefruits and mandarins can only be grown, of course, in areas that

are frost-free or nearly so. However, some of the newer varieties of mandarins (tangerines) can be grown where the temperatures go down to 25°F (−4°C).

The varieties of citrus trees all have different mature sizes and you must rely on your nurseryman for one to fit the location you have selected. They all share, however, the trait of requiring very little pruning as mature plants. In fact, because citrus trees store energy in their leaves, removing leaves will reduce the plant's capacity to ripen fruit.

One variety, the Meyer lemon, is definitely bush in form and requires almost no trimming: perhaps just a little heading back to keep it in the space or shape that you want. Most of the other varieties of citrus may be purchased on dwarf root stock and handled like the Meyer lemon. All of these plants, either standard or dwarf, should have the side limbs pruned off to give a short trunk, perhaps 24 to 30 inches from the ground. This pruning gives a rounded head but keeps the limbs out of contact with the ground even when they are loaded with fruit.

Fig trees
Because a fig tree bears fruit on one year or older wood, pruning is necessary only to shape a tree for its health and convenient picking. Prune figs to suit the growing situation. Different varieties grow in different ways. The California Black and the Adriatic grow like a spreading shrub. Do not head

these trees back, for they will never grow tall or wide. Select scaffold branches at the first dormant period and prune to keep future branches off the ground. Each year, remove low branches that touch the ground or interfere with picking.

The Kadota fig is a vigorous grower that should be kept low-headed and spreading. Head new growth short in the middle of a tree and longer on the outsides. When a tree reaches its mature shape, head new growth back to 1 or 2 feet.

Pear trees
You should train the young pear tree to the modified central-leader system by selecting 5 or 6 scaffold branches over a two-year period. Since it is characteristic of pear varieties to grow upright, be careful not to have too many heading-back cuts for that will promote too many upright shoots. If you want a small pear tree, buy a dwarf; don't try to make a standard smaller by heavy pruning.

The pear is very susceptible to fire blight, especially in the soft succulent growth that results from heavy pruning, so you must be careful about heading back or thinning shoots

on mature trees. Once fire blight takes hold, there is very little you can do about it.

Peach trees
Most newly planted young peach trees are pruned to the vase or open form. When the tree is planted, it is cut off at between 24 and 30 inches in height and 3 or 4 of the laterals are left to grow into vase form. These should be headed back the second year only, and only if they exceed 28 or 30 inches in length. These laterals should be spaced evenly around the trunk and 6 to 8 inches apart vertically.

The peach tree after the second year should be pruned lightly. Heavy pruning will result

in a weak tree. During the second and later years, the object is to prune for an open center or bowl-shaped tree. This requires that all branches other than the main 3 or 4 be removed from the trunk and the vertical rising shoots on the remainder be pruned off. Your ultimate goal is to have a wide tree with an open top 12 to 14 feet high. As the tree grows, cut the upward growing foliage back to outward growing laterals.

When the tree reaches 10 or 12 feet and is maturing, start cutting back the new growth on the top of the tree severely, being sure to maintain the open center that will admit light to the lower inside parts of the tree. Generally, pruning should be lighter on young bearing trees than on older peach trees.

Plum trees
Plums fruit on wood produced the previous year and on spurs on older branches. They are particularly prone to branch splitting when mature and bearing heavy crops. Prune all plums in the winter when dormant.

There are many plum varieties but they can be examined as two groups; the Japanese and the European. The latter includes prune trees.

Japanese plums
Most of the dessert plums you'll find at the market are in this group—for instance, the Santa Rosa and Satsuma. Some grow upright and some spread out; but all fruit of trees in this group is borne on stubby spurs no longer than 3 inches. These spurs will bear for from six to eight years.

Remove one-third of the new wood each year by thinning and heading. This heavy pruning is necessary to produce larger fruit. Keep long, thin branches headed to shape a tree into a stubby, wide form.

When the fruit spurs on a branch have borne for six or eight years, select a new branch from lateral shoots on this branch. The following year, remove most of the old branch, cutting it off just above the selected lateral.

European plums
This group of plums includes the prune, which is a plum whose high percentage of sugar allows it to dry without fermentation. Prunes are left on the tree until they fall or are shaken loose.

The main distinction between European and Japanese plums is the length of the fruiting spurs; the European fruit spurs may reach 3 feet, much longer than the 3-inch spur of the Japanese type.

Since the fruit buds are so spread out, far less fruit thinning is needed and the long

bushlike mass of spurs does not require the severe pruning given Japanese varieties.

Quince trees
The peculiarity of a quince is that it bears fruit only on a short growth from the buds that flower at the tips. Fruit is borne only on soft wood emerging from year-old wood. New growth

originates in lateral buds on the previous year's growth.

The quince tree tends to be small and bushy. Keep it thinned and open at the top. Remember, since fruit grows at the tips of new growth, branches cut back too far won't bear.

Walnut and pecan trees
The walnut tree is so naturally beautiful that it is often used as an ornamental tree. It is one of

the few trees that grows large even without pruning.

If you want a good crop of walnuts, though, you can do some things to help a tree's production. (The same techniques can be used to increase pecan production.)

The young walnut tree from the nursery is unusually tall — 7 to 8 feet — and thick-trunked, but it should be cut back to 4 feet in height or to 3 to 5 buds. In summer, select a single, vigorous shoot to train as the leader, staking it securely because it will be soft and brittle. Pinch back all other shoots.

The first dormant season, head back the leader to the closest vigorous bud. This will stimulate the laterals. In the second winter, select a first scaffold branch high enough off the ground — about 6 feet — that you can walk under it easily. As the tree grows, select other scaffold branches to radiate around the trunk about 20 inches apart.

Laterals that develop on new scaffold branches usually grow out at undesirably narrow angles. Remove such laterals and select new ones from buds the following year; they will produce wider-angled crotches.

Mature, bearing walnut trees that are trained properly will require little pruning other than thinning to allow light to penetrate the crown. Low or crisscrossing branches and diseased or broken wood should be regularly removed.

Shrubs

An encyclopedic guide to more than 70 species of the most commonly planted shrubs. What is the difference between pruning deciduous and broad-leaf evergreen shrubs? When do you prune them? How do you train a hedge?

Pruning shrubs

Renewal is the key word regarding the pruning of shrubs. Most of our best flowering shrubs, if not periodically thinned by cutting the oldest wood to the ground, will decline into a sparse flowering thicket.

How do you know when to prune your shrub? By knowing which of the two basic types it is. The first type blooms in the spring on last season's wood. The second type blooms in summer or fall on wood formed the same year. There are several minor exceptions, such as some clematis that blooms twice and some shrubs — flowering quince, for example — that bloom on wood which is one or more years old.

Spring flowering shrubs bloom on wood grown during the previous season. Forsythia is an example. It can be pruned while in bloom if you want to have flowers for the house. Or it can be pruned immediately after blooming. But if you cut forsythia too much later than this, after the flowering wood has grown, you will be cutting off the unborn flowers of next year.

Summer or fall flowering shrubs bloom on the current season's wood. An example is the summer lilac, *Buddelia davidii.* You have a pruning choice here: prune shrubs in this group either after flowering or wait until early spring — after frost is no longer a possibility. Be sure to prune early in spring before new growth starts.

Left: Hedging is one of the more familiar uses of shrubs in a landscape. They may vary in height from a few inches to several feet. Right: Some gardeners use a string as a guide to maintain a level hedge top. It can also be done by the method of the man who is cutting to a heighth measured by the top of his ladder.

Pruning deciduous shrubs

Remove long shoots that spoil the shrub's shape. Cut off only part of the new growth, leaving several buds, or cut to an unflowered lateral.

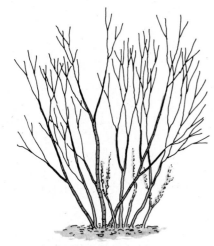

Remove all branches or branch laterals that lie on the ground as well as all broken, diseased, dead, or crisscrossing branches.

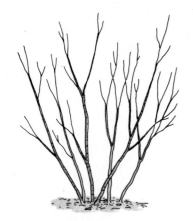

Thin out about one-third of the oldest branches, leaving no stubs.

Shrubs are either **deciduous** or **evergreen**. If deciduous, they lose their leaves in winter. Of course, evergreen means leaves are retained throughout the year.

There are degrees of being deciduous or evergreen. A shrub may be evergreen in a warm climate and deciduous, or partly so, in a cold one. Also, because a plant is called evergreen does not mean it never loses its leaves. It will drop and replace leaves more or less continually rather than all at once.

Many people equate evergreen with conifers, the needle-leaved and cone-bearing plants. But larches are deciduous conifers (see page 36). Conversely, all broadleaf shrubs are not deciduous.

Pruning deciduous shrubs

Deciduous shrubs are a group of plants that have the unique ability to renew themselves almost indefinitely. Some shrubs growing in eastern gardens are alive and healthy after more than a century. Yet these plants don't appear to be more than five years old. The secret is proper pruning. Let's examine two basic approaches: the three-year system and the five-year system.

The three-year cycle

Each year a deciduous shrub produces many shoots from the plant's base or roots. Decide on the size you want the shrub to be to fill the available space. Then prune so that a third of the shoots will be one year old, a third will be two years old, and a third will be three years old. After blooming, cut out most of the three-year old wood. Cut these shoots at the ground. Doing this will induce new shoots to spring up, leaving the desired number to form first-year shoots the following year.

The only other pruning necessary is to reduce the total height of the shrub to keep a plant within the bounds that you want. Removing the third-year wood every year after blooming will guarantee that you will always have young, healthy wood to produce the best new flowers.

A bonus of the three-year system is a healthier plant. Older wood is more susceptible to insects or disease than are young and strong shoots.

The five-year cycle

Using this pruning approach, you follow the same steps as in the three-year system but spread them over a five-year period. This longer system is used with such slower-growing shrubs as lilac and some viburnums. Keep in mind that you will not get as many new shoots each year in this method as you do in the three-year system.

Don't overprune

Once you learn the general rules for pruning all shrubs, it is time to consider the exceptions. Various ways to prune individual shrubs are listed at the end of this chapter. But keep in mind this general rule: *don't overprune.* Here are some cautions:

☐ Some shrubs do not like to be pruned at all. An example is daphne, unless you want to cut flowers for indoors. Another is the witch hazel, *Hamamelis mollis*: it has a permanent framework that isn't easily replaced.
☐ Slower-growing shrubs don't need much pruning because they can keep a permanent framework as they grow. An example of such a shrub is the star magnolia, *Magnolia stellata*.
☐ Pruning should aim at a natural effect. Overpruning — even in the interests of neatness — will destroy the individual irregularity that distinguishes each of nature's species from the others.

The most usual offense committed against a shrub is to shear it into a shape that its growing nature will not let it keep. A laurel hedge is an example of a shrub that won't tolerate shearing. If you do shear it, you cut across the broad large leaves and the hedge looks ragged. Soon the leaves turn brown and look even worse.

Another example of overambitious pruning is to strip away a shrub's lower branches. Although doing this keeps the ground underneath looking neat, the absence of lower branches produces an odd appearance. An example is the forsythia: cut old branches to the ground but leave the short bottom ones to fill out the lower silhouette.

In general, prune only as much as is necessary to maintain the health of the plant and to restore dying, flowerless branches.

Pruning broad-leaf evergreen shrubs

Broad-leaf evergreens should be pruned in the same way as deciduous shrubs, except for those that are slow-growing. Slow growth usually results in a neat, compact form but the interior leaves dwindle as the shrub matures, producing a hollow dome.

A special group — rhododendrons and azaleas — is discussed in the next chapter.

As with any group of plants, the evergreens need occasional pruning: cut away a branch that outgrows the rest; remove broken, dead or diseased branches; and shape back if the plant is encroaching on its neighbors or covering a window.

Late fall is often the best time to prune the broad-leaf evergreens. Pruning at this time will open the plant, cut down on fungus and make the plant easier to spray against over-wintering diseases.

In areas where subzero temperatures and high winds can be expected, late fall pruning could open up the shrub to windburn of the suddenly exposed inner leaves and open cuts. This can contribute to an excessive loss of moisture (called desiccation), a danger that can be reduced by adequate mulching.

Pruning hedges

Plants used as hedges are types that can tolerate heavy pruning. When you plant a hedge, you must start intensive pruning right away. An important step is to discourage gaps from developing at the bottom of the hedge. The only way to prevent this is by pruning, but pruning *before* the hedge grows too large.

Start young

Buy hedge plants that are bare root or in gallon size cans. Space plants 24 to 30 inches apart and shear off about a third of the sides and tops. Shape them smaller at the top than at the sides. Shearing forces thicker growth right down to the ground; the wider base allows the sun to reach the bottom foliage. Without shearing or shaping, the inevitable result will be a hedge that has no leaves at the bottom and gaps throughout. Unpruned hedges also have a loose, uneven texture and generally look messy.

Trimming the new hedge once, though, is not enough. You must trim it back 3 or 4 inches at least three or four times a year for the first two years. Don't try to achieve the hedge height you want the first year. Keep shearing until the hedge is thick, with no gaps, before you let it grow to the desired height. Though this may sound demanding, it is the only way to train a young hedge into a satisfactory mature one.

Mature hedges

Hedges can be trained into either formal shapes or informal shapes. Of course, certain species of shrubs make better formal hedges, and others can only be informal because of their growth pattern and leaf size.

Since formal hedges must assume smooth architectural shapes, they require small-leaf, close-textured plants. Boxwood, lavender and rosemary traditionally have been formally shaped because they respond so well to close, repeated pruning. Larger-leaf, more open shrubs — such as cotoneaster and lilac — can only make informal hedges and should be pruned, not sheared.

Flowering shrubs — when to prune them

Spring blooming shrubs
Shrubs that bloom in the spring on last season's wood:
Prune them after flowering.

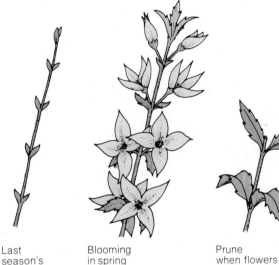

Last season's growth   Blooming in spring   Prune when flowers fade   New growth develops during the summer

Summer blooming shrubs
Shrubs that bloom in summer or fall on wood formed during the spring: *Prune them in early spring.*

Last season's growth   Prune in early spring before new growth starts   New growth develops in late spring and summer   Blooms develop on new stems

Starting a hedge

Gallon-sized cans of hedge plants are best to start with. Plantings can be about 18 inches apart. Prune off about one-third of the top and sides.

Prune off one-half of the new growth every two months through the growing season.

Shape the hedge narrower at the top so sunlight can reach the bottom foliage. Repeat this process until the hedge reaches the desired height.

Alphabetical list of ornamental shrubs

Listed here are the most popular ornamental shrubs. The list is arranged alphabetically by both the botanical name and various common names. If a shrub has no common name, it is listed only under its botanical name.

All specific pruning information will be found under the botanical name, in three categories: *Characteristics,* which tells if a shrub is deciduous or evergreen, and how it grows; *How to prune; When to prune.*

A plant may have many common names but it can have only one botanical name. For example, the shrub *Viburnum opulus* is also known by the following common names: Cranberry bush, European cranberry bush, Guelder rose and Whitten tree. Thus, if you've been calling your bush a "cranberry bush," you'll find it so listed and will be directed to *Viburnum opulus.*

Abelia grandiflora
(Glossy abelia)
Characteristics: Evergreen but may lose some leaves when temperatures drop. Will reach 10 feet high and 8 feet wide. Small leaves are glossy, tinged purple in winter. Small pink flowers produced in clusters midsummer to fall. The cultivar 'Edward Goucher' is similar but lower-growing, has finer texture and larger flowers.
How to prune: Flowers usually formed on previous season's wood but in a long season the new spring growth is most floriferous. Can be sheared at expense of some flowers and beauty. Best when selectively pruned. Pinch most vigorous new growth in spring, remove one-third of oldest growth annually.
When to prune: Do major pruning in winter, control pruning in late spring.

Abutilon hybridum
(Chinese bellflower, Chinese-lantern, Flowering maple)
Characteristics: Tender evergreen grown primarily for hanging. Has bell-shaped flowers, large maplelike leaves. Relatively fast growing to 5 or more feet high and wide. This is a fine indoor tree, excellent for a sunny window.
How to prune: Growth tends to be somewhat scraggly — occasional tip pinching helps maintain density. Can be cut back one-third or more every winter if a smaller plant is desired. Periodically replace oldest branch with a sucker. Otherwise remove suckers as they appear. Can be trained as standards, espaliers and shrubs.
When to prune: Do major pruning in fall or early spring, pinch during growing season.

Acer palmatum
(Burgundy lace, Japanese maple)
Characteristics: This much loved small tree is available

in cultivars that seldom reach over 10 feet high. 'Burgundy Lace' is a common one that has finely cut leaves and reddish foliage.
How to prune: Main consideration is to maintain umbrellalike shape. Remove crossing and wrong-way branches. Thin excessive inside growth which appears occasionally and train upward to promote layered effect. Usually multitrunked, low branching. (For pruning as a tree, see *Acer palmatum* in Chapter 4.)
When to prune: When dormant, early spring.

Allspice
see *Calycanthus* species

Arbutus unedo
(Cane apple, Strawberry tree)
Characteristics: Evergreen, grows slowly usually to 12 or so feet but may reach as high as 20. A relative of manzanita, its tiny white flowers have the familiar bell shape. In fall, red strawberrylike fruits (edible but bland) hang from the branches. Multistemmed. It also shows a handsome reddish brown and scaly bark.
How to prune: Usually grows into interesting shapes naturally. Remove lowest branches in time to reveal bark. Crown may become too dense and need to be thinned. Shearing tolerated but is not the best method.
When to prune: In spring before newest growth.

Arctostaphylos manzanita
(Common manzanita, Parry manzanita)
Characteristics: Other manzanita species and cultivars are catching up on the common one. It is a treelike shrub native to California coastal ranges. Evergreen. Variable size of 6 to 20 feet high, to 10 or more feet wide. Naturally develops an interesting form and is sometimes used as decoration. Smooth, reddish bark; white, drooping, bell-shaped flowers.
How to prune: Requires little to none. Prune to reveal bark. Pinch most vigorous growth to prevent legginess.
When to prune: Before new growth in spring, or anytime.

Arundinaria
see *Bamboo*

Aucuba japonica
(Japanese aucuba, Japanese laurel, Gold-dust plant)
Characteristics: Evergreen shrub which grows moderately fast to 5 to 10 feet but height can be easily controlled. Large 7-inch leaves. Many variegated forms available with speckled

leaves. A dioecious plant. It is most valued for ability to grow in heavy shade.
How to prune: Check upright shoots if they become floppy by heading back, clipping just above new bud.
When to prune: Winter for major work if necessary. Spring is best for limiting growth.

Australian fuchsia
see *Correa pulchella*

Azara microphylla
(Boxleaf azara)
Characteristics: A 10- to 18-foot tender evergreen native to Chile. Yellow flowers fragrant with a scent reminiscent of vanilla (to most people). Needs shape and plenty of water.
How to prune: Remove shoots with spent flowers in late spring. It is handsome when trained against a wall, whether formally espaliered or not. Prune to outside laterals to control height. Occasionally, replace an old trunk with a new sucker.
When to prune: Anytime is all right for most work. Major cuts should be before new growth in spring.

Bamboo
Characteristics: The several genera of the bamboos included here have essentially the

same pruning methods. All are members of the grass family but range in height from a few inches to 100 feet. There are two basic distinctions between bamboos: some spread with underground rhizomes and some spread by expanding clumps.

Arundinaria	rhizome
Bambusa	clump
Chimonobambusa	rhizome
Dendrocalamus	clump
Phyllostachys	rhizome
Pseudosasa	rhizome
Sasa	rhizome
Semiarundinaria	rhizome
Shibataea	rhizome

Most common are *Bambusa multiplex riviereorum, B. m.* 'Golden Goddess' and *Phyllostachys aurea.*
How to prune: Clump growers can be sheared for use as a hedge and should be thinned occasionally. Use rhizome types with discretion — they're equally beautiful but frequently become more of a weed than a desirable plant. Root pruning is a big job but it's necessary to contain them. Or bury an 18-inch barrier of a material (metal, concrete, plastic) that won't decay around them. If you're living happily with the taller types, prune them up, removing leaves for two-thirds of their height.
When to prune: Spring is best but anytime is all right.

Barberry
see Mahonia aquifolium

Beautybush
see Kolkwitzia amabilis

Beloperone guttata
see Justicia brandegeana

Berberis thunbergii
(Japanese barberry)
Characteristics: Deciduous shrub that grows to about 5 feet high and as wide. Nearly round leaves turn red before falling. Red berries hang on, sometimes throughout winter. Very thorny. One of the best hedge plants. Many cultivars available, some of deeper color and others of more compact, consistent growth.
How to prune: Can be sheared to make formal hedge although this is not the preferred method. Better to let them grow naturally, thinning and pinching to maintain size and shape. Renew by removing old wood to the ground.
When to prune: Anytime is all right but hardest pruning should be done before new growth in spring. Pinch after flowering.

Bigleaf hydrangea
see Hydrangea macrophylla

Black-alder
see Ilex

Blue barberry
see Mahonia aquifolium

Border forsythia
see Forsythia intermedia

Box
see Buxus microphylla

Boxleaf azara
see Azara microphylla

Boxwood
see Buxus microphylla

Bridal wreath
see Spiraea

Broom
Characteristics: Brooms include members of three different genera: *Cytisus, Genista*

and *Spartium.* Though the plants differ in many respects, culture of all is similar. They range in size from small garden miniatures to spreading shrubs. Most brooms are excellent plants for hot, dry, sunny locations, though they may be difficult to get started.
How to prune: Cut back one-third, being careful not to cut into older, leafless wood because old stems rarely will sprout. For the same reason, old twiggy specimens are difficult to rejuvenate.
When to prune: Right after flowering.

Buddleia davidii
(Butterfly bush, Orange-eye buddleia, Summer lilac)
Characteristics: Fast growing to between 7 and 15 feet. Dies to the ground each year in cold winter areas, semievergreen where warmer. Coarse leaves. Small white flowers on branch tips in August. The many cultivars available vary primarily by flower color.
How to prune: Cut to ground each year if frost doesn't do it for you. It will flower on current season's growth.
When to prune: After frost in fall or before new growth in spring.

Burgundy lace
see Acer palmatum

Butterfly bush
see Buddleia davidii

Buxus microphylla
(Box, Boxwood)
Characteristics: The varieties or cultivars, which vary only slightly, are most frequently planted. All have small leaves of rich green and are frequently used as sheared hedges of nearly any size up to 3 or 4 feet.
How to prune: If shaped hedge is desired, begin pinching the

leading growth of the young plants to produce maximum number of branches. Will form a handsome but more casual looking hedge if left alone.
When to prune: Late spring to maintain shape.

Calico bush
see Kalmia latifolia

Callistemon citrinus
(Crimson bottlebrush, Lemon bottlebrush)
Characteristics: Most common and easily grown bottlebrush is evergreen, grows to about 12 feet. Three-inch long leaves are bronze colored at first, change to flat green. Red flowers are tiny but cluster along stem like a bottlebrush.
How to prune: Adapts to several training methods — small tree, espalier, multitrunked shrub. Best flowering is gained by cutting back a little each year. As with pines, cut only in leafy parts of stem to avoid baring branches which may then die.
When to prune: In winter or just after flowering.

Calluna
see Heath and Heather

Calycanthus species
(Allspice, Carolina allspice, Pineapple shrub, Spice bush, Strawberry shrub, Sweet shrub)
Characteristics: Deciduous shrubs that grow to about 10 feet high and 7 feet wide. Coarse leaves have sandpaper-like surface, when crushed are aromatic.
How to prune: Natural habit is to develop several stems close to the ground. To keep small, pinch during growing season. Occasional thinning and trimming to shape is necessary.
When to prune: Thin in fall or spring before new growth begins. Pinch to shape anytime.

Camellia
Characteristics: Much favored and widely used evergreen shrubs. All require partial or full shade. Of the main species, *C. japonica* is most common, *C. reticulata* has the largest flowers and *C. sasanqua* takes the most sun, heat and cold. Useful as accents, screens or informal hedges. Over 3,000 varieties are available varying in form, size, color and climate adaption.
How to prune: Maintain shape by taking two or three leaves with the bloom when cutting flowers. Save one bud of a cluster, make a small hole in the others by piercing from the tip of the buds downward. Air enters and these buds will dry and fall. Start shaping when young to encourage domi-

nance of a single stem with many branches. Frequent pinching thereafter will keep pruning problems to a minimum. Size can be drastically reduced over period of two seasons: before new growth begins, remove lower three-fourths of branches to force buds to break along length of stem; in the following spring, top to desired height. Insure healthy root system necessary for this process by fertilizing and mulching.
When to prune: Anytime tolerated but major work should be done in early spring.

Cane apples
see Arbutus unedo

Carolina allspice
see Calycanthus species

Caryopteris clandonensis
(Hybrid bluebeard)
Characteristics: Deciduous shrub sometimes treated as a perennial. Stays low, usually below 4 feet. Highly favored for the intense blue flowers that appear in late August.
How to prune: In colder climates, usually freezes to the ground each year. If not killed back naturally, it is best to cut back to within a few inches of ground, forcing maximum new growth. Flowers borne on current season's wood.
When to prune: Late fall or early spring.

Ceratostigma willmottianum
(Chinese plumbago, Willmott blue leadwort)
Characteristics: Evergreen or semievergreen and tender, grows to 4 feet high and as wide. Tolerates poor soil. Bright blue, 4-lobed flowers borne throughout summer.
How to prune: Cut back annually to promote best flowering.
When to prune: Early spring before growth begins.

Chaenomeles
(Flowering quince)
Characteristics: Deciduous, growing to 6 feet high and as

Deutzia scabra
(Deutzia)

Deutzia is a late spring flowering shrub that will look better and produce a more beautiful show of flowers if it is pruned annually. After the flowers fade, cut back the flowering shoots. The oldest stems should be removed every other year. Always cut to outward facing buds to improve the shape and to keep the center open.

wide. Likes full sun. One of the earliest of the spring-flowering shrubs in shades of red, pink or white. Flowers open before leaves appear. Many varieties available.

How to prune: Start training when still young to half-dozen or fewer main branches. Thin tangled center of older neglected quince by removing oldest stems gradually over three seasons. Flowers borne on wood of one year or older. Well-budded branches removed in winter can be forced indoors.

When to prune: When dormant is all right but summer pruning promotes formation of next season's flower buds.

Cherry laurel
see *Prunus laurocerasus*

Chimonobambusa
see *Bamboo*

Chinese bellflower, Chinese-lantern
see *Abutilon hybridum*

Chinese plumbago
see *Ceratostigma willmottianum*

Chinese witch hazel
see *Hamamelis*

Common lilac
see *Syringa vulgaris*

Common manzanita
see *Arctostaphylos manzanita*

Correa pulchella
(Australian fuchsia)
Characteristics: Wide-spreading, tender evergreen grows to 2 feet high and 8 feet wide. Only the flower is similar to *Fuchsia* — appears from November to April. Color is a tint of pink.
How to prune: No complicated problems: pinch most vigorous growth to induce branching and greater density.
When to prune: Anytime.

Corylus avellana
(European filbert, European hazel)
Characteristics: Ten- to 15-foot deciduous shrub with nearly round 4-inch leaves. Interesting male flower catkins hang all winter. The cultivar 'Contorta,' with its picturesque, twisted branches, is one of the most popular.
How to prune: Can be trained as a small tree or multitrunked shrub. If single trunk is desired, select strongest stem when young and remove suckers as they appear. If left as a shrub, occasional thinning is very beneficial.
When to prune: When dormant.

Cotoneaster
Characteristics: These are plants of many forms ranging in height from several inches to 20 feet. Most are evergreen but many are deciduous. Of the rose family, their flowers are white or pinkish; reddish or black fruits are borne in the fall. Generally vigorous growers needing little maintenance.

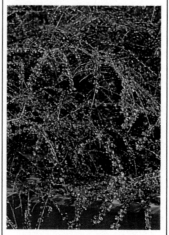

How to prune: Low growers may need dead wood removed occasionally. Don't shear them along an edge as branch stubs will remain unattractive for some time. Taller-growing types are frequently sheared into geometric shapes but look best when natural, fountainlike shape is emphasized. All are susceptible to fire blight disease — remove scorched looking dead branches, cutting well into healthy wood; then disinfect pruning shears. Old wood readily sprouts.
When to prune: Early spring or as necessary.

Cranberry bush
see *Viburnun opulus*

Crimson bottlebrush
see *Callistemon citrinus*

Cytisus
see *Broom*

Daboecia
see *Heath and Heather*

Daphne odora
(Winter daphne)
Characteristics: Spreading evergreen grows to about 4 feet high and slightly wider. Thick glossy 3-inch leaves are pink to red. Very fragrant flowers and popular for that reason but not the easiest plant to grow.
How to prune: Normally just cutting flowers to take indoors is the only and best pruning needed. Make cuts close to buds that face the direction you want growth to take: upward and out to form spreading shrub; inward facing to stimulate more vertical growth.
When to prune: After flowering in spring.

Dendrocalamus
see *Bamboo*

Deutzia scabra
(Deutzia)
Characteristics: A hardy flowering shrub and one of the taller-growing of the *Deutzia* genus. Height can reach 10 feet. Leaves are about 3-inch ovals with scalloped edges and rough to the touch. Flowers come in mid to late spring in clusters and are white, slightly tinged with red.
How to prune: This tall grower needs an annual going-over to prevent scraggly looks. Every five years or so, cut it nearly to the ground if necessary to rejuvenate. Best treatment is to cut back flowering stems about one-half way to the base each year. Flower clusters come from the wood of last season's growth.
When to prune: After flowering.

Dodonaea viscosa 'Purpurea'
(Hopbush, Purple hopbush)
Characteristics: A fast-growing native of the southwest U.S. that excels with very little maintenance. Untrained will develop into a dense 10- to 15-foot high shrub, and grow nearly as wide. Frequently seen as a small single-stemmed tree. Narrow leaves 4 inches long and distinctly purple, especially when grown in full sun.
How to prune: Given room, this shrub will require little or no attention. However, it can be sheared to fit a restricted space. When training to a small tree, select the most promising stem when young and direct all growth its way by continually pinching the shoots that form along it. As this trunk gains strength, the lower sprouts can be removed.
When to prune: Early spring before new growth.

Dwarf myrtle
see *Myrtus communis*

Dwarf winged euonymus
see *Euonymus alata 'Compacta'*

English laurel
see *Prunus laurocerasus*

Erica
see *Heath and Heather*

Escallonia species
(Escallonia)
Characteristics: Temperate climate evergreens frequently used around home landscapes. Valued for both their glossy, always clean looking foliage and flowers that are not dramatic but consistent. They hybridize easily and thus many cultivars and hybrids are available.
How to prune: Not a demanding shrub but will get leggy if

ignored for any length of time. Tolerates shearing and is frequently used as a formal hedge, but many people feel a less formal clipping is more attractive. Remove dead flower clusters. Always prune back to a branch or a visible bud.
When to prune: Anytime is all right but before spring growth will promote the best flowering.

Euonymus alata 'Compacta'
(Dwarf winged euonymus)
Characteristics: A deservedly popular hedge plant: it's hardy (well below zero), becomes a brilliant scarlet color in the fall and requires only semiannual clipping to maintain a neat hedge. An additional identifying characteristic is the bark on the twigs which forms corklike ridges.
How to prune: Shear to desired shape when necessary. Selective tip pruning creating a more informal hedge is also effective.
When to prune: Early spring and then again in midsummer depending upon growth rate and your standards.

Euonymus fortunei
(Winter creeper)
Characteristics: The hardiest evergreen of all. It can be formed as a spreading or climbing vine or shrub. Dark green leaves are about 2 inches long and have scalloped edges.

How to prune: Considerable annual pruning is most beneficial. Responds well to shearing and so is frequently used as a hedge. Remove dead wood (check to see if caused by euonymus scale, a common pest). It is sometimes rejuvenated by severe cutting back.
When to prune: Early spring is best. Avoid pruning in late fall because the new growth so stimulated may become a victim of frost.

Euonymus japonica
(Evergreen euonymus)
Characteristics: More upright-growing than *E. fortunei* and well regarded for being a tough shrub. One of the least hardy

euonymus, it is widely used in the southern states. Susceptible to mildew. Many cultivars are available.
How to prune: Usually about 10 feet high as a shrub but it can be pruned up and trained as a small tree. Keep thinned, allowing good air circulation if mildew tends to be a problem. Tip prune to maintain compactness.
When to prune: Major cutting back should be done in early spring. Light pruning is all right from late spring to midsummer.

European cranberry
see Viburnum opulus

European filbert, European hazel
see Corylus avellana

Evergreen euonymus
see Euonymus japonica

Exochorda racemosa
(Pearlbush)
Characteristics: A commonly available, slow-growing flowering shrub that is at its best in the colder sections of the country. In time, it becomes vase-shaped and about 12 feet high. White flowers open from pearllike buds in May.
How to prune: These may become somewhat leggy so occasionally cut back branches about halfway. Remove faded flowers. Rejuvenate by cutting one-third of the oldest wood to the ground every three or four years.
When to prune: After flowering or when dormant.

False hop
see Justicia brandegeana

Fatshedera lizei
(Fatshedera)
Characteristics: An evergreen shrub commonly used in the warmer climates. Glossy 7-inch leaves have 3 to 5 pointed lobes. Trained upright, a height of 4 feet is usual. It has a slightly greater spread. Though tough, it is often a houseplant.
How to prune: To maintain as a bushy shrub, clip growing tips frequently. Equally satisfactory as a ground cover or vine (an espalier, for instance). It is possible to start over too: cut to the ground and new growth will appear.
When to prune: Anytime is all right but early spring before new growth is best for major work.

Flowering maple
see Abutilon hybridum

Flowering quince
see Chaenomeles

Forsythia intermedia
(Border forsythia)
Characteristics: Fast-growing (to 6 feet or more) deciduous

shrub valued for its very early display of yellow flowers. In some climates, the bare branches are covered with flowers as early as February. Usually, nurseries offer named varieties such as 'Beatrix Farrand' and 'Lynwood Gold.' Flowers grow on last season's growth.
How to prune: Once mature, begin annual removal to the ground of about one-third of the oldest wood. Tip tallest branches as desired to maintain shape. If suckers become excessive, remove most of them, but leave some to replace the removed stems.
When to prune: After flowering. Remember that budded branches can be forced to bloom indoors as early as December.

Fragrant olive
see Osmanthus fragrans

French hydrangea
see Hydrangea macrophylla

Fuchsia hybrida
(Fuchsia)
Characteristics: Popular flowering shrub, standard, or hanging basket. Thrives in coastal, frost-free climates but grown in all climates. Soil should be light and porous. Use lots of water and fertilizer.
How to prune: Remove most of last season's growth annually. Standards need periodic thinning to prevent tangling. Hanging baskets should be pinched two or three times before flowering starts.
When to prune: In cold climates, after first frost and again in spring back to live wood. Early spring only in frost-free climates.

Genista
see Broom

Glossy abelia
see Abelia grandiflora

Gold-dust plant
see Aucuba japonica

Guelder rose
see Viburnum opulus

Hamamelis species
(Witch hazel, Chinese witch hazel, Japanese witch hazel, Vernal witch hazel)
Characteristics: Tall-growing deciduous shrubs (some to 30 feet but usually half that or less) native to many parts of the world. They are planted for their out-of-season display. The leaves are colored in the fall and unusual flowers show up in very early spring or, in some climates, winter. Flowers are fragrant, small, usually yellow and have petals that look like a small piece of crumpled ribbon. Witch hazels are relatives

of the commonly planted tree, American sweet gum, *Liquidambar styraciflua.*
How to prune: *Hamamelis mollis* doesn't like to be pruned. With other types, when desired height is reached, begin pinching back the most vigorous growth. If you want, train a witch hazel into a small tree with a single trunk: select the strongest stem when young and continue pinching side growth and removing suckers until desired height is reached. Then remove branches along the trunk and prune crown to shape.
When to prune: In winter, take branches to force into flower indoors. Otherwise, prune in late spring and summer.

Heath and Heather
Characteristics: These include the *Calluna, Erica* and *Daboecia* genera. All grow best in similar environments — cool and wet. They are fine-textured and, when in flower, covered by many small, red to white bell-shaped flowers. Once established, they're tough, low maintenance plants. Rooting is close to surface. Flowers are long-lasting when brought indoors.
How to prune: In early spring, cut back to remove flower stalks and to stimulate dense growth.
When to prune: Before new growth begins in the spring.

Heavenly bamboo
see Nandina domestica

Hebe species
(Shrub Veronica)
Characteristics: A group of fairly tender evergreen shrubs native to New Zealand. Generally fast-growing, they're most popular for neat foliage and reliable growth: a common hedge plant. Tiny flowers in dense clusters are usually white but may also be purple.
How to prune: Remove faded flowers and seed capsules to reduce the drain on the plant's energy. Pinch new growth to keep compact. The shrub will

sprout if cut back to old wood. You can also rejuvenate an unkempt hedge by removing one-half of the old wood.
When to prune: If these shrubs are of borderline hardiness in your area, don't prune after midsummer. Otherwise, prune early spring and summer.

Highbush cranberry
see Viburnum opulus

Holly
see Ilex

Holly barberry, Holly mahonia
see Mahonia aquifolium

Hopbush
see Dodonaea viscosa 'Purpurea'

Hortensia
see Hydrangea macrophylla

House-blooming mock orange
see Pittosporum tobira

Hybrid bluebeard
see Caryopteris clandonensis

Hydrangea macrophylla
(Hydrangea, Bigleaf hydrangea, French hydrangea)
Characteristics: Very popular flowering shrub that has been cultivated for many centuries.

There will be no flowers when grown in climates with minimum temperatures that dip below 0°F. because flower buds formed the previous season are killed.

They can reach 12 feet but 5 to 8 feet is more common. Individually, the flowers are small but the clusters measure up to 10 inches in diameter. Flowers may be white, pink, red, or blue. Blue flowers are promoted by acidic soil.
How to prune: Neglected, hydrangea tends to become thin and woody with just an umbrella of foliage above the stems. Best handled by cutting back stems that have flowered to about 2 feet from the ground. Cut every cane back in this way to rejuvenate nonflowering specimens.
When to prune: Late spring when flowers have faded.

Hydrangea paniculata 'Grandiflora'
(Panicle hydrangea, Peegee hydrangea)
Characteristics: A very hardy and vigorously growing and flowering shrub. It's deciduous and can grow to 30 feet if trained as a tree. Develops large clusters of flowers that appear in late summer and hang on the plant into fall. Their color is white and sometimes purplish pink.
How to prune: An adaptable plant, it can be used as a tree or hedge. If overgrown, prune severely, leaving 3 or 4 main branches about 2 feet off the ground. To maintain as a hedge, clip back the fastest growing shoots frequently early in the growing season. As a tree, cut back annually, leaving branch stubs a few inches above where branching begins.
When to prune: Early spring.

Ilex
(Holly, Black-alder (deciduous), Possum-haw, Winterberry, Yaupon)
Characteristics: The hollies are a large group of plants widely varying in size and habit. Most are evergreen, the most notable exception being *I. decidua.* They have been so widely used for so long there are now as many as 150 different species of *Ilex,* over 200 cultivars of English holly, *I. acquifolium,* and over 1,000 of American holly, *I. opaca.* Heights range from foot-high ground cover to trees over 70 feet tall. Leaves vary but often are glossy, leathery and spined on the edges. The berries they set in the fall and carry through winter are a favored characteristic. Most hollies are what botanists call "dioecious," which means they need a mate to set berries.
How to prune: There are three basic growth habits of the hollies: pyramidal tree, rounded and dense shrub, and the open-growing border shrub. Read about the tree hollies in Chapter 4. The dense growers such as *I. cornuta* and *I. crenata* are often sheared. Cut back their new growth to shape. The open growing *I. verticillata* is best helped by periodic removal of its oldest canes to ground level.
When to prune: Anytime will do. Except where subzero temperatures can be expected, shear the hedges in midwinter to enjoy most of the berry crop indoors. In subzero temperature areas, shear before new growth starts.

Indian hawthorn
see Raphiolepis indica

Ivy, Ivy bush
see Kalmia latifolia

Japanese aucuba
see Aucuba japonica

Japanese barberry
see Berberis thunbergii

Japanese laurel
see Aucuba japonica

Japanese maple
see Acer palmatum

Japanese pittosporum
see Pittosporum

Japanese privet
see Ligustrum japonicum

Japanese rose
see Kerria japonica

Japanese skimmia
see Skimmia japonica

Japanese snowball
see Viburnum plicatum

Japanese witch hazel
see Hamamelis

Juniperus
(Juniper)
Characteristics: Among the most widely used and toughest evergreens. There are many species and cultivars from inches high to 50 feet. They survive and grow in heat or drought that would doom other plants. Because of their variability, there's a juniper to fit nearly every landscape need.
How to prune: If you are training young junipers, limit their growth however much you want by cutting back the newest growth almost to its point of origin. Cut above a side shoot that's heading in the proper direction. Will tolerate shearing but that causes trouble in the long run. Occasionally, thin topmost branches to

prevent their shading lower leaves.
When to prune: Anytime but spring or early summer is best.

Justicia brandegeana
(False hop, Shrimp plant)
Characteristics: Evergreen spreading shrub. Grows in a

mound to 3 or 4 feet but can reach 8 feet when well-adapted. Bronze, overlapping flower bracts surround the flower.
How to prune: Remove one-third of all wood annually after bloom. Pinch new growth to encourage bushiness.
When to prune: Heaviest pruning should be done after new growth in the spring. Pinch during late spring and summer.

Kalmia latifolia
(Calico bush, Ivy, Ivybush, Mountain laurel, Sheepkill, Spoonwood)
Characteristics: Hardy ever-

green, native throughout many of the mountain areas of eastern North America. Relatives of rhododendrons and require similar growing conditions such as acidic soil and partial shade. They will, however, grow on a drier summer site than rhododendrons. Grow to 25 feet maximum but usually much less — around 10 feet. Tiny white or reddish flowers are held in 5-inch clusters in early spring.
How to prune: See rhododendrons in Chapter 7.

Kerria japonica
(Kerria, Japanese rose)
Characteristics: Hardy deciduous, flowering shrub that grows to about 8 feet with an open, rounded form. Twigs remain green all winter. Leaves bright green and coarsely veined. Handsome flowers come in late spring. They're yellow, about 1½ inches in diameter and look like simple rose flowers. There are cultivars available.
When to prune: Flowers are borne on growth of previous season so cut back canes that have flowered — or are weak and growing slowly — to where new buds are visible or to the ground.
When to prune: After flowering, in late spring.

Kolkwitzia amabilis
(Beautybush)
Characteristics: A hardy de-

ciduous shrub that grows in an arching or vaselike way to 10 or 12 feet. Pink flowers are profuse in late spring. They mature into delicate brown, hairy seed clusters that may remain until the next spring. Attractive tan colored bark is like thin cork and peels in flakes. The beautybush has also been used effectively as an informal hedge or screen.

How to prune: Best practice is to cut a few of the oldest canes to the ground each spring. Flowers are developed on the growth of the previous season. To prune a neglected specimen, first remove most of the suckers (leave a few of the best as replacements) and the growth from ground up to about 5 or 6 feet. Then select the oldest or weakest canes and remove them. If the crown is still a tangled mass at this point, thin it.

When to prune: After flowering, in late spring.

Laurus nobilis
(Laurel, Sweet bay)
Characteristics: Can be either a shrub or tree. It is the laurel that the Greeks used to make wreaths for scholars.
How to prune: See Chapter 4.

Lemon bottlebrush
see Callistemon citrinus

Ligustrum japonicum
(Privet, Japanese privet, Wax-leaf privet)
Characteristics: A reliable evergreen shrub popular in temperate climates. Makes excellent screens and hedges. Unchecked, it could grow to 12 feet or more but is usually kept much shorter. Leaves are about 3 inches long and colored a lustrous dark green. Privets need little attention unless they form part of a formal hedge. When training to hedge form, clip often through summer to build up a strong and wide base. Periodically, remove oldest wood from the base.
How to prune: Do any major cutting in early spring before new growth begins. To maintain form, prune anytime.

Lilac
see Syringa vulgaris

Lily-of-the-valley bush
see Pieris japonica

Ling
see Heath and Heather

Magnolia stellata
(Star magnolia)
Characteristics: One of the lowest-growing magnolias, often no taller than 10 feet. It's a native of Japan and an excellent accent when used near entryways or anywhere it can be seen close up. Flowers appear in very early spring before the leaves. They're white, fragrant, about 2½ to 3 inches wide and have several petals. Improved cultivars are available.
How to prune: As is true of the tree magnolias, the star magnolia requires very little pruning. Watch when young so ill-placed branches can be removed when they are as small as possible — magnolias are very susceptible to wood diseases that get into large wounds.
When to prune: Anytime is all right. Usually all the pruning necessary can be done when the shrub is in flower. Then the trimmings can be used indoors.

Mahonia aquifolium
(Barberry, Blue barberry, Holly barberry, Holly mahonia, Mountain grape, Oregon grape)
Characteristics: A hardy evergreen native throughout wide areas of northwestern U.S. and British Columbia. The state flower of Oregon. Grows to 6 feet high or more but lower-growing varieties are available. Leaves are leathery and spined somewhat like a holly. During winter and early spring they have a coppery tint. Lemon yellow flowers are held in spikes above the leaves in spring, later maturing into blue-black berries. It spreads with underground roots.
How to prune: As plant matures, it develops several stems that are virtually bare of leaves except at the very top. Remove these stems right to the ground and the plant will remain bushier. Pinching new growth after flowering also encourages bushiness.
When to prune: Remove whole stems before growth starts in the spring. Any pinching back or light pruning to control size can be done in spring or summer.

Mirror plant
see Griselinia lucinda

Mock orange
see Philadelphus coronarius and Pittosporum

Mountain grape
see Mahonia aquifolium

Mountain laurel
see Kalmia latifolia

Myrtus communis
(Myrtle, True myrtle)
Characteristics: This is the plant so frequently referred to in ancient literature. It's evergreen and grows to 5 or 10 feet high. You'll recognize (or never forget) the fragrance of the leaves if you have the happy chance of crushing them in your hand. Not very resistant to cold but is very tolerant of heat, drought and seacoast conditions. A dwarf myrtle, the cultivar 'Compacta,' is denser and low-growing.
How to prune: Malleable is the word for this plant. Leave it to form an irregular mound or shear it in any way you can imagine. If you want to reduce its height, do it from the inside out. Reach in and clip off the tallest stems from inside the plant.
When to prune: Anytime will do but to maintain formal hedge, after first growth in spring and again in midsummer.

Nandina domestica
(Heavenly bamboo, Sacred bamboo)
Characteristics: Usually an evergreen but it will lose leaves as temperatures approach zero. Similar to bamboos in many respects but not even related to them. In fact, it belongs to the barberry family. It grows slowly to 6 or 7 feet. Small, pale white flowers in spring develop into red berries in clusters by fall. Fruiting is increased if several plants are grouped.
How to prune: Nandina will grow quite happily with no attention at all but will look best with annual thinning. Choose 3 or 4 old canes and remove them to the ground. To maintain at a constant height, continually pinch new growth at the top.
When to prune: Anytime is all right, but best before new spring growth.

Orange eye buddleia
see Buddleia davidii

Oregon grape
see Mahonia aquifolium

Osmanthus fragrans
(Fragrant olive, Sweet olive, Tea olive)
Characteristics: A fairly tender evergreen shrub with tiny, almost insignificant flowers that

Nandina domestica
(Heavenly bamboo, Sacred bamboo)

These feathery leaved shrubs have clearly become overgrown. They shade out lower leaves, and the entire plant has a scraggly look. High branches are headed back to lower growing younger shoots. Some are completely removed to reduce competition. This rejuvenation pruning will result in a lower, more compact, attractive plant.

release pervasive sweet fragrance into summer evenings.
How to prune: No matter how trained — as a tall shrub, tree, hedge or espalier — some pruning is needed to maintain shape.
When to prune: If used as a hedge, shear it first in early spring, then later on as needed. Frequent pinching of new growth will help develop good form.

Panicle hydrangea
see Hydrangea paniculata 'Grandiflora'

Parry manzanita
see Arctostaphylos manzanita

Pearlbush
see Exochorda racemosa

Peegee hydrangea
see Hydrangea paniculata 'Grandiflora'

Philadelphus coronarius
(Mock orange, Sweet mock orange)
Characteristics: This species is probably the most popular (or at least best known) of a large group of species and hybrids. Most are deciduous, hardy, vigorous growers valued for their flower display in spring. Similar to *Deutzia*, requires like care.
How to prune: Flowers are borne on the wood of last season's growth. For that reason, annual pruning that promotes the best new growth also promotes the best flowering the next year. Remove one-third or less of the oldest canes to the ground each year.
When to prune: After flowering in spring.

Photinia fraseri
(Photinia)
Characteristics: A photinia notable for the attractive deep red of its new leaves. When growth spurts in early spring, the entire plant may be this color. Later, some leaves green up and plant is attractive two-tone. It is a fairly tender ever-

green and grows at a moderate rate to around 10 feet. Mildew resistant.
How to prune: Train to many stems while young. Pinch the most vigorously growing stems. Clip back two or more times per season to keep new leaves coming as well as maintain shape.
When to prune: Late spring and summer. Don't prune too late in summer if you live in the coldest areas that this plant can tolerate.

Phyllostachys
see Bamboo

Pieris japonica
(Lily-of-the-valley bush)
Characteristics: This leathery-leaved shrub is one of the best flowering evergreens for the north country. A blueberry relative, its flowers have the characteristic upsidedown-urn shape and are arranged in clusters. It can, in time, reach 8 to 9 feet high and about half as wide. Several cultivars are now available, selected for either compactness or flower color.
How to prune: These are easy to manage plants that need very little pruning. Remove faded flowers and any developing seeds. Pinch the new growth of a specimen that's become too leggy.
When to prune: After flowering.

Pineapple shrub
see Calycanthus

Pittosporum
(Australian laurel, Mock orange, Pittosporum)
Characteristics: Bearing **poisonous** orange berries, these are temperate climate evergreens much praised by gardeners for their toughness and reliability. Most were imported from Australia or New Zealand although one of the best, *P. tobira,* was brought from China and can bloom indoors.
How to prune: Although some grow tall, becoming tree size if left alone, nearly all the pittosporums can be pruned and held at any height. These are often used as hedge plants, sheared or selectively clipped for a more formal look. *P. tobira* is best trained to an open, multistemmed shrub that emphasizes its natural habit.
When to prune: Anytime.

Possum-haw
see Ilex

Privet
see Ligustrum japonicum

Prunus laurocerasus
(Cherry laurel, English laurel)
Characteristics: English laurel

is a very useful evergreen native to Europe and long cultivated there. Where climates are warm and seasons long, it may reach 30 or more feet, elsewhere much less. In colder areas, this is one of the best broadleaf evergreens for hedging but it will not survive subzero temperatures. In warmer climates it grows very fast, requiring frequent shearing. Flowers come in summer, are white and hardly noticeable. The cultivar 'Schipkanensis' is slower growing and somewhat more hardy. 'Zabeliana' has more drooping branches that can be espaliered or even pegged down as a ground cover.
How to prune: Benefits from annual pinching of top growth. Prune to desired shape.
When to prune: Spring through midsummer.

Pseudosasa
see Bamboo

Raphiolepis indica
(Indian hawthorn)
Characteristics: These are leather-leaved shrubs of such

undemanding culture and predictable behavior that they are one of the most beloved to mild-climate landscapers. They flower profusely over the winter, then set blue-black fruits. The species is not grown much because of the variability of its seed. Many cultivars are available that vary by flower color or height. For example, 'Balerina' stays around 2 feet high while 'Bill Evans' may reach 7 feet.
How to prune: Really very little pruning is required. Pinching two or three times per year will encourage dense growth.
When to prune: Anytime, spring through summer.

Rhododendron
see Chapter 7

Sacred bamboo
see Nandina domestica

Sasa
see Bamboo

Scarlet wistaria
see Sesbania tripetii

Scotch heather
see Heath and Heather

Semiarundinaria
see Bamboo

Sesbania tripetii *(formerly Daubentonia tripetii)*
(Scarlet wistaria)
Characteristics: A fast-growing but short-lived relative of wistaria. Deciduous, it will grow to 10 feet high and nearly as wide. Beginning in spring and sometimes lasting through summer, dark orange wistaria-like flowers hang in clusters.
How to prune: Can be trained as a multistemmed shrub or small, flat-topped tree. To train to one trunk, choose strongest stem and continually pinch side growth, eventually removing it. Whether grown as a shrub or tree, you should thin it annually, shortening branches almost back to the main framework.
When to prune: When dormant or early spring, before growth begins.

Sheepkill
see Kalmia latifolia

Shibataea
see Bamboo

Shiny xylosma
see Xylosma congestum

Shrimp plant
see Justicia brandegeana

Skimmia japonica
(Japanese skimmia)
Characteristics: A slow-growing evergreen valued for its beautiful leaves, flowers and fruit. It spreads slightly wider than its height of about 4 feet. Thrives in the Pacific Northwest but not too well elsewhere. *S. japonica* is "dioecious," meaning two plants (a male and a female) are needed for berries.
How to prune: Very little needed. Pinch new growth to encourage denseness.
When to prune: Summer.

Snowball
see Viburnum plicatum

Spartium
see Broom

Spice bush
see Calycanthus species

Spiraea
(Spirea, Bridal wreath, many other forms)
Characteristics: Deciduous and hardy, these flowering shrubs are among the easiest to grow. Flowers are usually white but some are pink and even red forms are available.

How to prune: Since the flowers are the prime virtue of these plants, most pruning is done to encourage best flowering. Remember that most spireas flower on previous season's wood but some (usually those that bloom latest in the season) flower on current season's wood. The rule is therefore: if flowers formed on last year's growth, prune after flowering; if flowers formed on current year's growth, prune in early spring. Following is a list of those to prune in early spring (all others should be pruned after flowering):

S. albiflora
S. bullata
S. bumalda
S. 'Anthony Waterer'
S. bumalda 'Froebelii'
S. japonica
S. margaritae

Don't worry if you do not know the particular species you have. Simply wait, observe when the flowers appear, then prune accordingly the following year. Occasionally thin old, thick clumps by removing old canes to the ground.
When to prune: See above.

Spoonwood
see Kalmia latifolia

Star magnolia
see Magnolia stellata

Strawberry shrub
see Calycanthus species

Strawberry tree
see Arbutus unedo

Summer lilac
see Buddleia davidii

Sweet bay
see Laurus nobilis

Sweet mock orange
see Philadelphus coronarius

Sweet olive
see Osmanthus fragrans

Sweet shrub
see Calycanthus species

Syringa vulgaris
(Lilac, Common lilac)
Characteristics: Grown wherever winters get cold. Through the states of New England they are much beloved. They are deciduous multitrunked shrubs that can grow as high as 15 feet. Several hundred hybrids are now available. Called French hybrids, they usually have larger flowers of particular colors and may flower later in spring.
How to prune: Leave lilacs alone for the first few years (except to remove suckers that arise below a graft). Prune hard to renew an old specimen but go a little easier on a grafted plant. Remove dried flower heads. Flowers are formed on

previous year's wood.
When to prune: After flowering in spring.

Tea olive
see Osmanthus fragrans

True myrtle
see Myrtus communis

Vernal witch hazel
see Hamamelis species

Veronica
see Hebe species

Viburnum opulus
(Cranberry bush, European cranberry, Highbush cranberry, Guelder rose, Whitten tree)
Characteristics: A hardy deciduous shrub that grows 12 to 15 feet high. Flower clusters of spring are handsome but in fall the plant becomes a showcase. Leaves turn bright red before falling. Bright red fruits first show in late fall. Several cultivars are available, including the dwarf 'Nanum.'
How to prune: Little pruning is required. Periodically, thin oldest wood. Can be trained to a single trunk: choose the most likely stem when young and keep side shoots pinched until it reaches the height you want.
When to prune: Before new growth in the spring.

Viburnum plicatum
(Snowball, Japanese snowball)
Characteristics: Deciduous flowering shrub grows to about 10 feet. It is somewhat less hardy than V. opulus. Leaves are dark green, prominently veined and turn deep red in fall. This plant is grown for the round white flower clusters that appear in May.
How to prune: Little required, but can be trained into tree form.
When to prune: When dormant.

Wax-leaf privet
see Ligustrum japonicum

Weigela and Weigela hybrids
Characteristics: Strong-growing deciduous flowering shrubs.

At one time more popular than today. If you own one, it is likely an old specimen. Many varieties and hybrids are available that grow to a manageable 10 foot maximum but older types grow taller. Flowers are formed singly or in clusters on year-old wood.
How to prune: With attention (frequent pruning), can be kept to almost any size. Remove branches that have flowered back to a side branch. Remove oldest wood annually.
When to prune: Prune after flowers fade in late spring.

Whitten tree
see Viburnum opulus

Willmott blue leadwort
see Ceratostigma willmottianum

Winterberry
see Ilex

Wintercreeper
see Euonymus fortunei

Winter daphne
see Daphne odora

Wisteria

Witch hazel
see Hamamelis species

Xylosma congestum
(Shiny xylosma)
Characteristics: A very useful evergreen, sometimes a deciduous shrub. Very adaptable and one of the most drought tolerant shrubs. On its own, it forms an open, round, spreading plant about 10 feet high. Leaves are tough, shiny and a light yellow green.
How to prune: Though little pruning is necessary, prune as desired to expose trunks, train to a single stem for a small tree, espaliered, or even as a topiary.

When to prune: Any time will do but best to prune after the springtime growth surge to maintain shape. Any major pruning done in early spring will be quickly covered by new growth.

Yaupon
see Ilex species

This overgrown bush has been neglected for several years. The canopy was raised by pruning to upward growing branches. The tangle of branches was eliminated and center opened. Now the cranberry bush will be more attractive when it displays its maple-shaped leaves.

Rhododendrons and Azaleas

Basically, all you need are your finger tips
to prune most of this gloriously blooming group.

Prune a little, pinch a lot

Rhododendrons and azaleas require more grooming than pruning. The spent flower heads of rhododendrons should be removed — this is called "deadheading." Tips of azaleas should be pinched out to make the plants bushier. Be careful not to take next year's buds with the flower.

Your finger tips will do nicely for most of the pruning of this gloriously blooming group. Only older plants that have become leggy, sparse or damaged will require a few cuts from your hand pruners or loppers.

Before reading about care for these plants, you should understand that there is very little real difference between a rhododendron and an azalea. Size isn't an accurate way to judge which plant is which. In a nursery, rhododendrons tend to be larger and azaleas smaller. But in a specialty nursery, you might find dwarf rhododendrons only several inches tall, and in older gardens in the south, you will see azaleas as large as trees. Sizes of both plants vary from 8 to 80 inches.

If the difference between a rhododendron and an azalea isn't size, what is it? The difference lies in where buds are placed, and this causes them to need different types of pruning. Since rhododendron buds are always found

Left: An azalea close-up explains the popularity of this species. The delicate texture and subtle color gradations clearly enhance the charm of these favorites.

Right: A planting of rhododendrons and azaleas brings visual attention to the more shaded corners of the garden in each spring. They thrive in the filtered light of surrounding trees.

The difference between rhododendrons & azaleas

The difference lies in where the buds are placed, and this causes them to require different types of pruning. Azaleas (left) bloom on lateral axillary buds as well as terminals. Rhododendrons (right) bloom only on terminals. Since rhododendron buds are always found just above the leaf rosette,

you must cut there, just above the buds. On an azalea, the buds are concealed under the bark along the entire branch. Therefore, you can cut anywhere on a azalea, and still be near a bud. And that bud, in turn, will break into new growth.

Reducing the size of a rhododendron

To the left is a 7-foot plant, very thick, hanging over a walk. This landscape would benefit by a reduction in its size. To reduce the width and height, thin back side branches as shown in the illustration (right). If empty places

in the foliage result, they will fill in quickly. Such systematic reduction in the size of a rhododendron can also be applied to azaleas, camellias and other ericaceous plants.

just above the leaf rosette, you must cut there, just above the buds. On an azalea, however, the buds are concealed under the bark along the entire branch. This means that you can cut anywhere along the branch and still be near a bud, which will then break into growth.

One other difference is that evergreen azaleas can thrive in mild southern climates where rhododendrons are rarely found. For example, you will find many evergreen azaleas but few rhododendrons in southern California.

The major trouble with both rhododendrons and azaleas comes from faulty cultural conditions. If a branch is yellowing, looks limp or dies, you should cut it away. If the whole plant continues to deteriorate, then you can be certain that the soil is incorrect or that the plant is getting too much or not enough sun. Some varieties require sun, some require filtered shade and some take a fair amount of both sun or shade. Place the right rhododendron or azalea in the right light conditions, and many future problems will be avoided. In general, azaleas will grow in sunnier locations than rhododendrons. This is especially true of the deciduous group of azaleas.

Soil conditions are also vitally important for this group. Rhododendrons and azaleas require a loose soil, rich with humus. It must also be acid soil; alkaline soil kills them. If the soil is full of natural humus, it is also acid, since humus is always acid.

A third cultural factor, just as important for this group as pruning, is the way in which you plant them. Both rhododendrons and azaleas must drain quickly and have soil loose enough for air to penetrate. They must be planted in a watertight hole, and they must not be buried too deeply. The shallow roots must remain near the surface where air can penetrate and drainage is quick. Poor drainage encourages root rot, which becomes a very serious problem. Ideally, these plants like to be set slightly higher than the surrounding soil to insure this essential fast drainage. If you plant them this way, be sure to put an inch or two of loose humus over them so the sun doesn't dry out the roots lying close to the surface.

Oak leaf mold, sold by the bag at nurseries, is an ideal mulch. As it decomposes, it provides the perfect soil.

To sum up, rhododendrons and azaleas require very little pruning, particularly when young. But they do need the correct soil, correct planting and the right amount of sun or shade to stay healthy. The individual requirements of the three main groups are considered next: rhododendrons, evergreen azaleas and deciduous azaleas.

Rhododendrons

The first thing to learn about pruning a rhododendron is how to remove spent flowers. If seed pods are left on the plant, they consume much of the energy that could go into flowers or leaves. Hold the branch with the faded flower in one hand and with the other hand carefully snap off the flower head with a slight sideways pressure, taking care not to harm the growth buds below. These buds are next year's flowers and leaves. If you injure the flower buds, there will be no flowers next year.

If your plant is too tall to hand-pick thoroughly, little harm will be done. Try using a hose to wash the dead petals away.

Many rhododendrons tend to become alternate bloomers if they are not deadheaded.

Young rhododendrons, like young azaleas, should be tip-pinched to produce bushier plants. When they are older or if they have been neglected, several conditions make pruning necessary:

☐ The interior of the plant may have accumulated dead wood from loss of light inside the bush. This wood should be cut out, down to the first live rosette of leaves. If there aren't any rosettes, cut out the whole branch.

☐ The rhododendron may become too leggy, with all its leaves at the ends of the branches. A more subtle kind of pruning then becomes necessary. Even on rhododendrons, there are *some* growth buds under the bark. They are located where older leaf rosettes once existed, but since the leaves have fallen, they are hard to detect. Look closely, though, and you will see a faint ring and swelling where the fallen leaves once were. If you cut just above one of these, you will be cutting above a dormant growth bud. The cut will activate the bud and a branch will emerge at that point.

The best time to do this kind of pruning is in the winter in mild areas or in the spring where winters are severe. As mentioned earlier, the very best time to prune is right after the plant blooms. When pruning in winter or early spring, there's always a chance that you may be cutting off some future bloom.

One special caution for rhododendrons: cut off suckers on grafted plants because if left to mature, they will divert growth away from the graft. Cut them off cleanly where they emerge.

☐ An older rhododendron may have become overcrowded. This often happens when rhododendrons are planted as a loose hedge or screen. Prune to correct, but prune slowly. Do it over a period of several years, cutting to increase the interior light inside each plant. If this isn't enough, remove some plants; the remaining rhododendrons will go on increasing in size, filling in gaps.

As a last resort, replant. Since rhododendrons are shallow-rooted, replanting will give you a chance to raise their soil position. When you do, add some rich humus to the planting hole. Old plants sometimes sink into the ground, or the soil may become compacted. Replanting corrects these conditions.

Evergreen azaleas

Evergreen azaleas require less pruning than rhododendrons. They should be tip-pinched, particularly when young, to produce a bushier plant. Do this after the plant blooms.

When azaleas become older, stronger pruning may be necessary. Because of the distribution of buds along the entire branch, an azalea can be cut anywhere and so it can be sheared — although some people never shear an azalea because shearing destroys the natural shape. Shearing produces a crop of flowers at the sheared surface and all of the flower buds spring into action at the same time.

To rejuvenate an older evergreen azalea that has grown too woody and leggy, prune it over a period of two or three years. The first year, cut back the oldest branches to within 10 to 12 inches of the ground. The next year, do the same thing, and repeat this the third year. Never cut off more than a third of the plant each year. In this way, you can safely transform the azalea into a compact, bushy plant that will produce an astonishing crop of flowers.

Deciduous azaleas

Nothing can match the brilliant colors of the deciduous azaleas — flame, orange, deep yellow, purple or the variegated combinations of these colors. They should be pruned as rhododendrons.

Deciduous azaleas tend to become leggy, woody and unproductive. When you see this happen, it's time to eliminate whole branches. As the plant gets older, you'll find that eliminating older branches becomes an annual pruning job.

Cut the old, unproductive branches off at ground level. This will send energy into new branches and keep the plant renewed and productive, year after year.

Other members of the azalea family, such as *Azaleas leucothe* and garden blueberries, require very little pruning. Prune them only to keep them within bounds.

Deadheading

Remove faded flower trusses from rhododendrons by bending over and pulling gently. Be careful not to damage new buds.

To double or triple the number of flower trusses next year, pinch off about 1 inch of the sticky new growth when that new growth is about 4 inches long.

Two or three new shoots will sprout on each shoot you pinch. The second shoot here is now ready for pinching.

Roses

Pruning a rose might seem the
unkindest cut of all, but to leave a rose bush
unpruned would be far more unkind.
The general principle is: cutting off old wood
regularly produces new wood.

Produce new wood by cutting the old

To prune a rose — the most romantic
of flowers — might seem the unkindest cut of all. But to leave a rose bush
unpruned would be far more unkind.
Left alone, it would grow into a hope-
less tangle of thorns.

From all the differing instructions
on how to prune the various rose species, a comforting general principle
filters out: cutting off old wood regularly produces new wood. The energy
that would have gone into keeping the
declining old wood alive goes instead
into producing new wood and flowers.
When you save the plant's energy,
your reward will be bouquets of
beautiful roses.

The two rose groups

Regarding pruning, there are two
major groups of roses. One group
blooms on the current year's wood;
the other group blooms on last year's
wood.

Roses in the first group should
have all three-year-old wood removed.
This is the old wood that must be removed to hasten the emergence of
new, blooming shoots. Do it when the
plant is dormant.

The second group, which blooms
on last year's wood, should be pruned
after flowering and the emergence of

*Roses either close-up or in mass
are the acknowledged favorite
flower. They are tough and
adaptable to nearly every climate.
They respond with a profusion
of flowers to any extra
attention. Left, a grouping of
floribunda flowers. Right, the
climbing polyantha, Mme.
Cecile Brunner.*

Pruning pillar or rambling roses

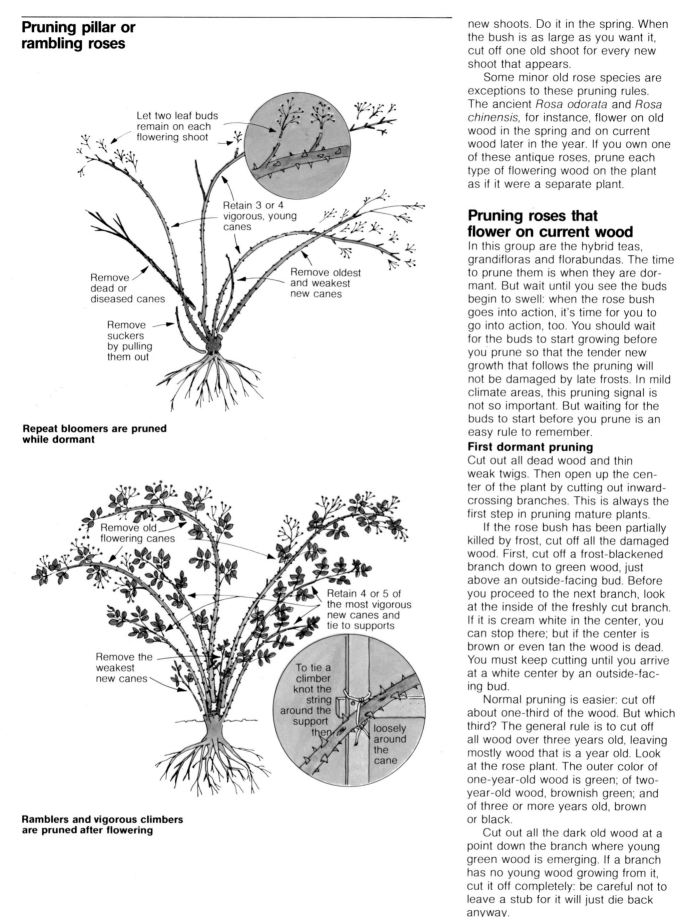

Let two leaf buds remain on each flowering shoot

Retain 3 or 4 vigorous, young canes

Remove dead or diseased canes

Remove oldest and weakest new canes

Remove suckers by pulling them out

Repeat bloomers are pruned while dormant

Remove old flowering canes

Retain 4 or 5 of the most vigorous new canes and tie to supports

Remove the weakest new canes

To tie a climber knot the string around the support then loosely around the cane

Ramblers and vigorous climbers are pruned after flowering

new shoots. Do it in the spring. When the bush is as large as you want it, cut off one old shoot for every new shoot that appears.

Some minor old rose species are exceptions to these pruning rules. The ancient *Rosa odorata* and *Rosa chinensis,* for instance, flower on old wood in the spring and on current wood later in the year. If you own one of these antique roses, prune each type of flowering wood on the plant as if it were a separate plant.

Pruning roses that flower on current wood

In this group are the hybrid teas, grandifloras and florabundas. The time to prune them is when they are dormant. But wait until you see the buds begin to swell: when the rose bush goes into action, it's time for you to go into action, too. You should wait for the buds to start growing before you prune so that the tender new growth that follows the pruning will not be damaged by late frosts. In mild climate areas, this pruning signal is not so important. But waiting for the buds to start before you prune is an easy rule to remember.

First dormant pruning

Cut out all dead wood and thin weak twigs. Then open up the center of the plant by cutting out inward-crossing branches. This is always the first step in pruning mature plants.

If the rose bush has been partially killed by frost, cut off all the damaged wood. First, cut off a frost-blackened branch down to green wood, just above an outside-facing bud. Before you proceed to the next branch, look at the inside of the freshly cut branch. If it is cream white in the center, you can stop there; but if the center is brown or even tan the wood is dead. You must keep cutting until you arrive at a white center by an outside-facing bud.

Normal pruning is easier: cut off about one-third of the wood. But which third? The general rule is to cut off all wood over three years old, leaving mostly wood that is a year old. Look at the rose plant. The outer color of one-year-old wood is green; of two-year-old wood, brownish green; and of three or more years old, brown or black.

Cut out all the dark old wood at a point down the branch where young green wood is emerging. If a branch has no young wood growing from it, cut it off completely: be careful not to leave a stub for it will just die back anyway.

Then cut two-year-old wood back about a third. Finally, cut the year-old wood — by about a third if it is strong and back to 2 or 3 buds if it is weak.

Make all cuts at outside facing buds in order to produce the classic vase shape of a well-pruned rose bush. The center will be open and the radiating branches will arch up and out.

Secondary or follow-up pruning
If the rose bush is new or weak, follow-up pruning should consist of no more than snapping off the dead flowers. The new bush needs all of its leaves to manufacture food.

Mature plants can be summer-pruned more heavily. As you remove spent flowers or take some fresh blooms inside for decoration, cut each stem so that you leave at least 2 sets of leaves on the branch (5 leaflets). At the minimum, cut the stem off just above the first outward-facing bud. Adjust your removal of flowers and the number of leaves to the general vigor of the plant. In this way, your summer pruning will seem no chore at all.

Pruning climbers
Most climbing roses flower on year-old wood. One group of climbing roses is known as "pillar" roses. The canes reach about 10 feet and you train them vertically. These are the climbing hybrid teas, climbing grandifloras and climbing floribundas. What do they have in common? Long, flexible canes that bear flowers all along their length. Don't prune them until they have reached the size you want. Then cut off dead wood and spent flowers.

The long canes are produced from ground level. Flowers appear the next year on the laterals of these canes. If new canes emerge, cut off an old cane for every new one that appears. If new canes do not appear, then cut the previously flowering laterals back to 2 buds.

Another group of climbing roses should be trained in fan shapes, for they require arching to flower well. These are the large flowered climbers and ramblers.

The reason for training in a fan shape is a condition in these roses known as apical dominance. Only the tips of the canes will grow and flower *unless* the cane is bent sideways. The tension along the cane produced by bending it encourages the dormant buds all along the cane to break into flower, a marvelous trick of rose magic.

Such large flowered climbing roses as the 'Don Juan' and 'Golden Showers' should be pruned a little differently because they flower on both old and new wood. New growth comes both from the base and from old canes. Flowers are produced from new canes and laterals, as well as from wood that is more than a year old. Prune laterals back to 2 buds after flowering; head back the new canes by a third.

About ramblers. These old roses produce long canes after blooming. Flowers will appear on these new canes the next spring only once but so profusely that many lovers of the rose still prefer ramblers to modern roses. You should prune rambler roses after flowering, when you see the new canes emerging. Cut off all old canes that are not producing new growth.

Since ramblers need constant heavy pruning and training every year, don't plant them unless you love them.

Pruning shrub and old species roses
Although these roses *can* be left unpruned, the result is unsightly. They usually become tangles of dead and diseased wood if neglected. Always perform pruning's primary step: cutting out all broken, crowded, dead and diseased wood. If roses are trained as single bushes, they will become large and will profit from an annual pruning after flowering. Open up the center, then the rest of the bush.

Many roses are grown as hedges, as boundaries or in back of lower flowering shrubs. In these cases, pruning has to take account of the shape and setting of the hedge. Content yourself with cutting off any long shoots that protrude excessively. Remove any old canes that no longer flower. If you prefer to be even lazier, wait until these old canes die so that you can easily spot and remove them.

Pruning specially shaped roses
Standard roses
Train this type of rose bush to a single trunk with the foliage 3 to 4 feet above ground. To keep the trunk single, rub off any sprouting buds that develop on it and remove any suckers at ground level.

The pruning aim here is to keep the crown symmetrical and the branches radiating evenly. Remove any parts that break this form, cutting branches back to an outward facing bud. An exception must be made when there is a gap in the crown; then prune to a bud facing toward this gap in order to fill in the space. Remove all rose hips and dead, diseased or twiggy wood. When necessary, retie the trunk to its stake.

Hedge and border roses
Vigorous and bushy roses make excellent hedges and borders. The small, pink Fairy rose grows into a profusely flowering border. Taller-reaching roses, such as 'Nevada' and many rugosa roses, make excellent flowering hedges.

Plant border roses about 2 feet apart and hedge roses 3 to 4 feet

Pruning a standard rose

Before

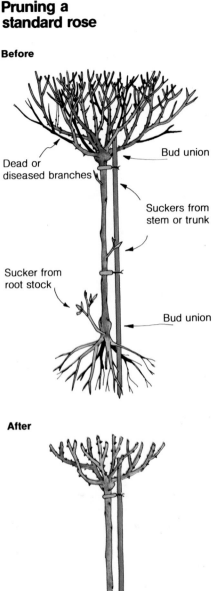

Dead or diseased branches

Bud union

Suckers from stem or trunk

Sucker from root stock

Bud union

After

Standard roses are pruned according to the same principles as bush roses. Cut out dead or diseased canes and prune healthy canes back to a good bud. Keep the center free from twigs and remove root and trunk suckers as they appear.

Pruning a hybrid tea rose

1

2

3

4

5

6

1) An unpruned hybrid tea rose

2) Remove any dead wood down to the nearest healthy dormant bud. Usually, it is necessary to cut at least one inch below the dead area.

3) Always cut until wood inside is healthy. Remove wood well past any evidence of disease. Healthy wood is creamy white, not brown or grey.

4) Cut out weak, spindly, or deformed twiggy growth. Remove canes growing towards the

center. If two branches cross, remove the weaker one. Remove rootstock suckers (where the growth originates from below the bud union).

5) Thin out the remaining canes, if necessary, and cut them to the desired length. In areas with the coldest winters, they may be cut back to an extremely short length.

6) Finally, apply a wound sealer to prevent the canes from drying out.

apart. Cut them back to 8 to 12 inches for bushy low-growing plants. Each winter, remove about half the new wood until the border or hedge reaches the desired height. Plants flowering on the current season's wood are pruned in winter; those blooming on older wood are pruned after flowering. Trim plants to a loose shape, as you would any informally shaped hedge.

Reviving old neglected roses

Contrary to popular belief, roses are very tough. On farms that have been abandoned for 50 years, sometimes the only plants found still growing will be asparagus and roses. The roses will probably be old varieties, rambler or shrub, but many of the newer hybrid tea roses also sink deep enough tap roots to last many years.

What is the first step in pruning an old, neglected rose? Remove all broken, dead and diseased parts; then prune away all weak, twiggy and inward-growing wood, and wood that is rubbing against another branch.

Open up the center of the bush by pruning to vigorous outward-facing buds. Cut back young wood to 2 to 3 buds. Fertilize and spray for fungus and insects. That's about all you should do the first year; to do more might send the plant into shock.

During the following dormant period, cut out an old branch at ground level. Reduce one of the remaining old branches by half and cut back two-thirds — not just one-third — of the new wood. Repeat this the next winter and the third winter, if necessary. You should end up with a rose bush that has no wood over three years old. Each year during revival pruning, you should see an increase in new wood and better quality roses. If not, you'd better dig up the old rose and replace it with a promising new one.

Right: An arbor of roughly cut timbers covered with an informal climbing rose at Old Westbury Garden in Long Island, New York — the essence of natural beauty.

Ornamental Vines

An encyclopedic guide to 21 species of the most commonly planted vines. How to control and direct their growth.

How to trim vines neatly

Vines that are not kept under control with yearly training and pruning can easily become unmanageable—almost beyond the help of pruning.

If a vine does seem hopelessly entwined, it may be best to chop it right down and start all over. When new shoots appear—and a mass of them will—select a third of the strongest and retrain them over the wall or fence. When new shoots have grown sufficiently long, tip them, keeping them restricted to the allotted space.

Thin the yearly crop of shoots to retain only the growth necessary to cover the wall or fence. Remove old shoots regularly; train the new ones into the empty spaces. If you prevent shoots from crossing or tangling too much, the vine will improve in foliage and flowers.

Usually, though, you can do something with old, neglected vines short of starting all over.

First, cut off all but 2 or 3 of the most easily traceable stems. Second, redirect these stems to grow over the space originally covered by the old vine. Then, cut back the laterals on these stems to 2 or 3 buds. The vine will quickly regain foliage and start producing better leaves and flowers.

Left and Right: These are the spectacular flowers of the genus, Clematis. Many species of varying color and growing habits are available; and most require different pruning techniques.

Planting and pruning vines

Vines usually do best planted at least 12 inches away from a wall or fence. The roots need room to fan out. If there's an overhanging roof, that's another reason to plant well away from the wall—to make sure that rain will reach the root area.

After you plant a vine, select 3 to 5 of the strongest shoots and reduce these to half their original length. This will encourage new growth to develop at the bottom of the vine and increase the vigor of the shoots that remain.

Like roses, ornamental vines flower in one of two ways: on the current season's growth or on the previous season's growth. In the former case, the vine should be cut back to a basic framework (or to the ground) during the winter.

In contrast, vines that bloom on the previous season's growth should be pruned after flowering. Remove shoots that have flowered or prune to a place on the shoot where new growth is emerging. So many new shoots will appear that you'll want to thin them, retaining only enough to fill the required space.

Vines that produce spurs—such as wisteria, the queen of all climbers—should have laterals cut back to 2 buds in the early spring before strong growth begins.

Trachelospermum jasminoides
(Star jasmine)

The Star jasmine is a summer bloomer that flowers only on new growth. Shear it before growth starts in the spring to encourage more new growth, and you'll have many more flowers.

Wisteria sinensis
(Chinese wisteria)

Prune off the tangle of flower stems, pods and any crowded or crossed side branches during the winter or early spring before new growth starts.

Leave only the flowering spurs and the permanent framework of the vine, the main stalks, and smaller branches that are growing in the direction you want them to.

Shorten the flowering spurs to a half-dozen or so buds to encourage larger flowers and separate, free-hanging clusters.

Alphabetical list of ornamental vines

The following list gives more specific information on how to prune each of the more popular vines.

Actinidia chinensis
(Kiwi berry, Chinese gooseberry)
Vigorous grower that needs regular attention. It can be pruned heavily; do major pruning when buds begin to grow. Old wood on established plants should be removed each year to encourage new shoots. Cut above strong buds directing growth.

Bignonia capreolata
(Scarlet trumpet vine, Trumpet flower, Cross vine, Quarter vine)
Woody vines that bloom on new growth; prune them in the winter. Watch out for many suckers; remove them as they appear. Cut spent, flower-bearing shoots each winter. (Prune these vines the same way: *Campsis, Clytostoma, Doxantha, Tecomaria*.)

Bougainvillea species
Another woody one. Prune after blooming, removing old weak-flowering shoots and cutting laterals back to 2 buds. A profuse flowering will result. Remove spent stems if frost damaged but wait until spring

before you do this; many apparently frost-killed shoots will suddenly show life in the spring.

Celastrus scandens
(Bittersweet)
Shrublike vine grown for its dried winter berries. The berries, however, are toxic, and should not be eaten. Its rampant growth will choke nearby plants. Prune regularly every winter, cutting out branches with spent fruit. Pinch out tips in summer. If a vine becomes too tangled or develops too many old branches, cut it to the ground in the winter; it will quickly sprout.

Clematis
five species:
    C. armandii After it blooms in spring, heavily prune this rampant grower by keeping only the stems you want and cutting out all others.
    C. jackmanii Flowers in summer on new wood. Prune after flowering, cutting to between 6 and 12 inches of the ground or, when young, to the first 2 or 3 buds.

    C. lanuginosa Blooms on old wood in spring and new wood in summer. Cut off laterals that have flowered to bring on the summer flowering.
    C. montana Vigorous vine. Prune it after it flowers. To keep

it from clambering to the top of its support and becoming top-heavy, train it horizontally. Prune old, tangled vines as buds start growing in spring. Cut out all nonproducing wood.
    C. 'Nelly Moser,' 'Romona' and 'Duchess of Edinburgh' All bloom in spring and again in summer. Prune as for *Clematis lanuginosa*.

Gelsemium sempervirens
(Evening trumpet flower)
Prune after flowering. This easily-managed vine can be heavily pruned, then will keep the shape you want with a general shearing.

Hedera helix
(English ivy)
Shear at any time in any way. This rapidly growing, long-reaching vine is very tough. Keep it from climbing a tree if you care for the tree because vine can eventually smother it.

Ipomea species
(Morning-glory)
Cut to the ground each winter and retrain in the spring.

Jasminum nudiflorum
(Winter jasmine)
Woody vine requiring little pruning. Flowers are produced on old wood. Prune after blooming, cutting off only a third each year in order to leave enough old, blooming wood.

Lonicera japonica
(Honeysuckle)
Prune this rampant grower after flowering by heading back and thinning mature plants. Remove all suckers and cut all stems that crowd unless you want to be swamped in greenery.

Parthenocissus quinquefolia
(Virginia creeper)
Stands any amount of shearing. If a vine is torn from its support, rupturing its suction pads, you must cut that part off; it will

never reattach itself. Prune away only dead or diseased sections.

Parthenocissus tricuspidata
(Boston ivy, Japanese ivy)
Prune as for *P. quinquefolia*.

Passiflora
(Passion vine)
Easily gets out of control, creeping over any nearby object by attaching itself with wiry tendrils. Watch it sharply when it is young. When it shows too much tendency to take over, you might as well cut this plant to the ground. Keep it sheared neatly, pruning in spring when new growth will quickly cover the cuts.

Polygonum aubertii
(Silver lace)
Delay pruning in freezing climates until spring. A fast, airy, light vine, it can be allowed to grow fairly unchecked. Then cut it to the ground or prune it back to a basic strand or two.

Solanum jasminoides
(Potato vine)
An evergreen vine with profusions of white clusters of flowers. Little pruning needed other than to keep it under control within the space intended.

Trachelospermun jasminoides
(Star jasmine)
Needs very little pruning. If it becomes too bare or produces fewer flowers, cut back old woody growth in spring to main branches.

Wisteria sinensis
(Chinese wisteria)
Let a young vine grow unpruned until it has reached the size you want; then cut back all new growth to the second bud in winter. In spring, cut out all streamers (leafless shoots) as they form. Prune laterals to 2 or 3 buds. Leave the spurs; they will be loaded with flower buds. In summer, cut off streamers and shorten laterals by half. Train main branches carefully, for they will become thick and heavy as the tree branches over the year; support them well.

Fruiting Vines and Shrubs

Strawberries are easy. Grapes and raspberries are more difficult. Here's how for blackberries, blueberries, boysenberries, currants, gooseberries, loganberries and red raspberries.

Little space, much fruit

Almost any fruiting vine or shrub produces many times its weight in edible fruit over the years. Even more remarkably, some vines—the clump strawberry, for instance—can perform this production miracle while growing in a few handfuls of soil. Some of these fruiting plants are as beautiful as anything in the garden. Heavily laden grape vines cascading over a shady arbor are not only productive but give beauty and shade.

How difficult are these small wonders to prune? Strawberry vines are easy; so are current and gooseberry bushes. Grapes and raspberries, though, require careful training for the first few years and regular pruning every year thereafter.

Strawberry

Let's take the easy one first—the strawberry. There are two types, the clump type and the more usual runner type. The European wild strawberry, *Fragaria vesca,* is a clump type that offers the ultimate in pruning ease: just pick the strawberries.

All newly planted strawberries, clump or runner, should have their blossoms removed until about the middle of July. Blossoms that appear later in the summer will produce a fall crop.

The more widely planted runner type of strawberry produces plantlets at the ends of runners. These runner plants form fruit buds in the fall and bear fruit the following summer. Pinching controls the number—which determines the size—of the berries. Pinching off *all* runners will produce a large

Strawberries are, for good reason, a home garden favorite. Choose a good variety and it can be harvested the first season.

Pruning five popular berries:

blackberries, boysenberries, loganberries, black raspberries and single-crop red raspberries

Last year's growth is blooming and bearing fruit as new shoots emerge from the crown (those shown near the ground). Remove all but 5 of the new shoots. Let them continue to grow on the ground.

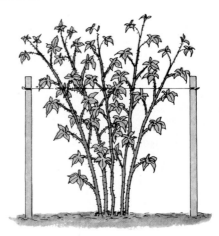

After harvest, cut *all* of the bearing canes to the ground and tie the 5 new canes to the wire.

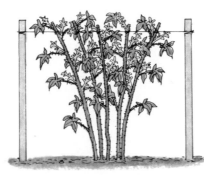

Head back the new canes at a point a few inches above the wire to encourage lateral growth along the wire.

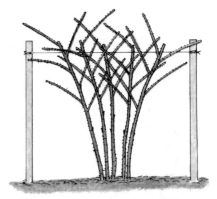

In winter, cut the laterals back to 18 inches. They will bear next summer and continue the cycle.

Strawberries

Strawberry runners are day-length responders and are sent out by the plant during the spring and summer growing season.

If you leave the runners on, you'll end up with multiple plants and more, but smaller, berries.

Pinch off the runners and you'll have single plants with larger berries.

plant and a few large berries. Allowing the plantlets to root and grow furnishes a larger crop of smaller berries.

Boysenberry, blackberry and loganberry

Since these berries are giant-step growers, pruning is the only way to keep them productive or even approachable. If you let them grow freely, you will soon have an impenetrable tangle. Prune them properly and they can be kept nicely under control.

All these berries grow in the same way; a cane develops from the crown and must grow a year before it can produce berries the second year. After producing berries, the cane becomes barren or dies. In either case, it should be cut off after you harvest the fruit. Thin new shoots to encourage no more than 4 to 5 of the strongest.

To train these berries, stretch a wire between posts 36 inches above the ground. Each year thin all but 5 of the canes. When they reach 30 inches or more, tie them to the wire and cut them off several inches above the wire. Laterals will soon emerge. In winter, cut these laterals back to 18 inches. They will bear the following year.

Meanwhile, let the selected 5 canes grow on the ground. When you cut the old canes off after harvest, tie the 5 new canes to the wire.

Allowing more than 5 canes to grow—or not cutting them back to

produce laterals — will tend to make the vine overbear and the fruit smaller and harder to pick.

Red raspberry

There are two kinds of raspberries: single crop and everbearing.

Cut the canes of single crop raspberries immediately after harvest. Train new canes onto a post or onto horizontal supports of wire or wood placed about 36 inches off the ground. In summer, as new canes grow, gather them in bunches. Thin out the weak shoots, tie the rest loosely together, and lay them along the ground until the old canes are cut; then tie the new canes to the supports. Head back any cane that outgrows its allotted space.

With everbearing raspberries, select 5 vigorous canes in the spring. Let these canes run along the ground until they reach 2 to 3 feet and tip

them to produce laterals. Cut off all the other canes. Tie the 5 selected ones to the supports and prune their laterals to 6 or 8 inch spurs. Do this during the dormant season. Such severe pruning makes berries grow larger.

Remember, the canes of both kinds of raspberries—single crop and everbearing—should be cut off after harvest.

Blueberry

The blueberry is a shrub, not a vine, but is handsome enough to be an ornamental. Blueberries are so hardy they can grow anywhere in the United States. However, since cross-pollination is essential for the production of fruit, more than one variety of blueberry must be grown.

The development of new, larger-berried hybrids has made the blueberry an increasingly popular plant. Very little pruning is necessary; the bushes need no wires or supports. Even though blueberries do tend to overbear, the fruit is small and light.

Remove canes that are three years or older in winter and thin out twiggy

growth. This is about all the pruning blueberries require. Adjust the number of old canes you remove each year by the size of the berries. If berries have been small, then prune more heavily that winter. If the berries have been large, you can safely do less thinning.

Currants

Though it's naturally a shrubby bush, the currant can be trained to a single trunk. But keeping 6 or 8 trunks will produce the maximum amount of large healthy fruit. Don't prune currents the first few years except for selecting the main shoots, eliminating suckers and lightly shaping the bush.

Fruit is borne on wood two or more years old but the best berries are found on two- and three-year-old wood. Keeping this in mind, remove the four-

year-old branches each winter. In summer, pinch new shoots to help shape the plants.

Gooseberries

Another of the shrubby, fruiting bushes, the gooseberry belongs to the same plant family as the current. Gooseberries bear both on one-year wood and on the spurs of older wood.

Two characteristics of the gooseberry are that it overbears and is subject to mildew. Thin a bush heavily to open it up. Because branches have very sharp spines, thinning will also

protect your hands and arms at harvest time.

At planting time, cut the young bush back to 6 shoots, retaining those that form an open vase shape. Remove shoots that touch or will eventually touch the ground. Bushes will bear a small amount of fruit the second year, but you'll have to wait until the fourth year for a generous crop. In the winter of the third year, cut away several of the branches, keeping the same number of shoots to replace them. After the fourth year, cut away *all* three-year-old wood (it will no longer bear) as well as some one- and two-year-old wood.

If renewal shoots do not appear, cut a three-year-old branch back to a

stub 4 to 6 inches long. The dormant buds on this stub will then grow. Thin these new shoots to keep the bush restricted to about 6 branches.

Although gooseberries demand heavy pruning, they will reward your attention with large berries, well worth the picking.

Grapes

All grape vines need heavy pruning to produce good grapes, particularly during the early years. When the vine is two years old, you must prune it in one of two ways, depending on the variety.

But one thing is true of all varieties: to produce large grapes with good flavor, you will have to sacrifice some of the grape bunches. For the first three years of training, allow only 6 to 8 bunches of grapes to mature; cut off the rest. From the fourth year onward, you may leave half the grape bunches on the vine.

From planting to the second pruning

Before you plant any grape vine, cut the roots to 6 inches and the stem to 3 buds. Bury the vine so that only the top 2 buds are above ground.

The first winter after planting, cut off all the new growth except for the strongest cane; cut that cane to 3 buds and tie it to a support.

Everbearing red raspberries

3½ feet high
Wire trellis hedge row

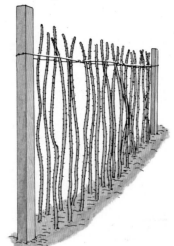

If you want your red raspberries to grow tall, they can be trained on a wire trellis hedge row. These will bear more, but smaller, fruit.

3 feet high
Unsupported hedge row

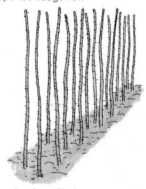

Red raspberries will also grow unsupported if they are shortened to 36 or 30 inches.

3½ feet high   3 feet high
Staked hill   Teepee

Two other novel ways to train these delicious berries are to tie them to a stake or make a kind of teepee formation. See text on opposite page for instructions on pruning.

Spur pruning of grapes

2nd summer
Head terminal
just above wire.

Leave only 2 laterals
near the top; tie them
loosely to the wire.

2nd winter
Leave only the first
bud on each shoot.

[Close-up of a lateral]

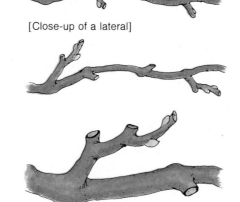

3rd winter
Spurs are 11 inches apart. Leave
two buds per spur.

4th winter on . . .
Prune off all but 2 buds at the
base of the strongest cane on
each spur.

The second spring, when sprouting shoots from the 3 buds are 12 to 14 inches long, select the strongest one from each bud and cut off all the others. Tie the three shoots to the support.

The second summer and beyond
The two methods of pruning mature grape vines are spur pruning and long cane pruning.

Spur pruning. Most European grapes, except for *Vitus-viniferra* (Thompson seedless), are spur pruned. These include 'Tokay,' 'Muscat,' 'Malaga,' and the California wine varieties.

During the second summer, stretch a wire between 2 supports at a 30 inch height. When a vine climbs about a foot above the wire, cut it back so that it's even with the wire. The top 2 buds will grow; train one along the wire one way, the other in the opposite direction. Tie each shoot loosely to the wire.

During the second winter, cut off all lateral growth from the 2 branches, being careful to leave the bottom bud on the remaining stubs.

During the third winter, thin laterals from the two main branches to strong shoots about 5 to 11 inches apart. Cut each lateral back to 2 buds or spurs.

From the fourth winter on, you'll find that 2 canes will grow from each spur and bear fruit. Leave the cane closest to the trunk on, shortening it to 2 buds. Cut the other cane off completely. Each winter, you should repeat this spur pruning; in that way, remaining canes will arch back toward the trunk each year.

Training of muscadine grapes

Continue to remove all shoots from the trunk each year unless you want to start a new plant by layering one of them.

Remove some entire spur clusters from the laterals to encourage new ones; cut others back to 2 or 3 buds.

Layering

These are the insect and disease resistent grapes popular for home gardens where temperatures stay above zero degrees Fahrenheit.

After planting, remove all shoots except one and cut it back to 2 strong buds. Establish trellis system, usually a single No. 9 wire 5 feet above the ground. Support posts should be 20 feet apart, the plants in between or near the posts. Train the first shoot up to form a straight trunk. Keep lateral growth removed. Remove growing tip when 3 inches above wire. Allow top 2 canes to follow wire in both directions.

During second winter, thin shoots to about 6-inches apart. Cut back canes growing from main lateral stems to 2 or 3 buds.

Fourth winter on, remove some of the entire clusters of fruiting spurs to maintain vigor and to allow new spur clusters to form. Prune heavily at the top of the trunk to prevent excessive growth there.

Cane training of grapes

2nd summer
Pinch off terminal about 1 foot above the top wire.

2nd winter
Cut through bud just above wires.

Leave 2 buds on each of 4 shoots nearest wires.

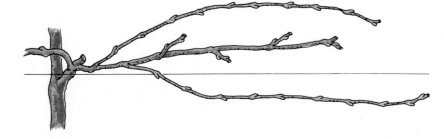

3rd winter
Leave 10 buds on each of the 2 basal shoots, 2 buds on each of 4 others. [Only 1 of the 4 branches depicted in the "2nd summer" illustration is shown here.]

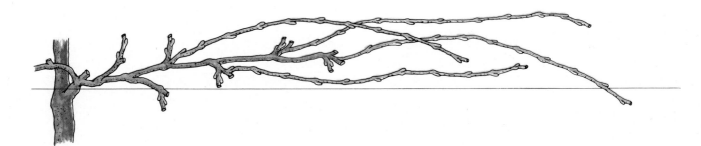

4th winter on . . .
Cut off fruiting canes to 2 buds.

Leave 1 fruiting cane (10 buds) and 1 spur (2 buds) on each of the 4 spurs.

Long cane pruning. This method of pruning is used for *Vitus-viniferra* and most American grapes, including the Concord and Delaware.

During the second summer, after you have trained the vine to a permanent trunk, stretch 4 wires between posts, 2 at a height of 2 feet and 2 at 4 feet. Pinch the top terminal shoot a foot above the top wire.

During the second winter, cut off the trunk right through the bud located just above the top wires. Remove all side shoots except for the 4 nearest each of the 4 wires. Cut back these shoots to 2 buds.

During the third winter, cut off all but 6 shoots. Leave 2 as fruiting canes with 10 buds. Cut the other 4 to 2-bud spurs.

From the fourth winter on, cut off the 2 fruiting canes. Each of the 4 spurs will have sent out 2 shoots during the previous year; cut the upper shoots as fruiting canes (leave 10 buds) and keep the lower shoots as spurs (leave 2 buds). Retain all spurs and 6 canes. Repeat this process each winter.

Green Art Forms

From topiaries to espaliers, cordons, pleaches, parterres and knot gardens there is a wonderful creative range of green art forms. Here are some basics.

Topiary — an elegant touch

After you've pruned the last tree, vine or shrub into the shape you like, you may want to apply your pruning shears to a more creative project. Topiary, the carving of shapes out of greenery, is a fanciful kind of sculpture that provides a surefire garden conversation piece.

You can shape individual trees and shrubs into birds and beasts. You can espalier shrubs against a wall in various patterns, make dwarf fruit trees into fruiting fences, pleach (interweave) branches into shady arbors, or create architectural fantasies out of living trees and call them gazebos.

A whole garden can be shaped into sculpured forms. In the French style known as "parterre," low borders of boxwood are planted and kept in formal patterns that fill the central garden space. The English "knot" garden is also created with low borders of two differently colored shrubs (gray and green) that interweave in a pleasing pattern or knot.

A French invention that later came to England and to early America is the "maze." Green hedges are planted in patterns that allow people to enter the maze but become confused by the intricate network of passages. A clever person can reach a secluded resting place at the maze's center. Lovers especially seem to like this green game.

Is all this a little too exotic? Certainly, entire gardens of topiary are suitable mostly for large estates or at least for people devoted to endless

Left: A dark green wall like this one of juniper makes a dramatic contrast to the statuary.

Right: The classic English knot garden of the public gardens at Hampton Court, Middlesex, England.

pruning. On the other hand, any venturesome gardener can create individual pieces of sculptured topiary, espalier fruit trees on walls or interweave branches into shady arbors.

Such a large yet specialized subject as topiary really requires a book of its own to describe how to construct each of the various forms. In this book on pruning, topiary has been kept as the final course, the dessert.

Individual topiaries

The ideal topiary plant is evergreen, fine-textured and hardy. Start with young, 1-gallon plants with plenty of low branches that fill out the bush close to the ground. Like a hedge, a topiary should be broader at the base than at the top so that the entire plant will be well exposed to sun. The wide base also helps the plant survive damage from snow or storm.

The two trees most often used in creating individual topiaries are boxwood and yew. Yew is ideal, box is almost ideal. Various other plants with bigger leaves and looser texture are less suitable but holly, cypress and evergreen privet—generally unsatisfactory for complex forms—work well for more general shapes such as cones or spheres.

You must be patient to create a topiary of boxwood or yew. If you want to make a double-ball shape, plan on five years for holly or privet, ten for yew. If you want a squirrel or other animal or bird form, you will have to wait twice that time.

The easiest topiary to shape is the double ball or "poodle." After the lower ball is formed, select several strong branches and let them grow at least 2 feet above the first ball. Then strip the foliage off the bottom foot to form the separating stem and begin to shape the other foot of growth into a second ball.

Tie the emerging stems together with soft garden cord until they have grown firmly into place.

One of the fastest ways to create a topiary is to train a vine such as English ivy or *Euonymus fortunei*. Form the figure you desire with chicken wire, hardware cloth or some similar material, and then train the vine to grow over it.

Espaliering plants

Almost any tree or shrub that doesn't grow too rigidly upright can be espaliered—that is, trained against the wall in a symmetrical pattern. Flowering quince is handsome; cotoneaster and pyracantha have colorful berries that benefit greatly from this treatment. If you want to cover a large wall or fence, nothing is more attractive than an espaliered evergreen magnolia.

Fruit trees are among the most rewarding plants to espalier. The easiest is the apple. Fruit develops well on an espaliered tree because every piece is fully exposed to sun and air. And the heavy pruning required in espaliering induces larger fruit.

A word of caution: where summer temperatures reach 90°F (32°C) or more, heat from the wall will cook the fruit. In this situation, espalier a tree onto a free-standing trellis for better air circulation. In cooler summer areas, you can safely espalier against a south wall.

All shrubs should have 6 inches between them and a wall. Wire or wood supports fixed at that distance will allow room for both air and branches.

Let's take an apple tree and espalier it against the wall. Run horizontal wires at intervals of 18 inches across the wall. Plant a bare root whip, then cut it off at 18 inches, at or just below the height of the first wire. This will activate the 3 buds just below the cut.

The first summer, train the 2 side buds onto the wire, letting the top bud develop as a trunk. Tie the 2 side branches onto the wire so that the tips are lower. Rub off all growth from the trunk and tip the growth on the branches.

Cut the trunk off a little below the second 36-inch-high wire. This will activate another set of buds. Keep 2 buds for side branches and 1 for the trunk extension. Train these as you did the first set of buds. Cut the laterals on the branches on the first wire back to 3 buds. These will develop into fruiting spurs.

Continue training until 3 wires (or as many as you wish) are covered with branches. On the top wire there

Four espalier methods of training

Double cordon espalier

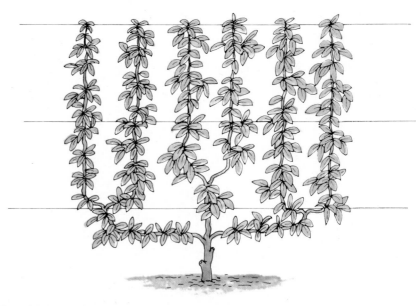

Candelabra espalier or
triple-u form

will be no trunk extension, just the 2 side branches.

Cordoning fruit trees

To cordon is a sure way to save space in the garden, and in the process, you'll create a living fence.

The difference between espalier and cordon (the word means rope) is in function. To espalier, you pattern plants against a wall or fence—usually one at least 6 or 8 feet tall. To cordon, you train fruit trees onto a low fence that stands away from any wall. The fence height is usually 3 feet, occasionally 5 feet.

A cordon fruit tree is trained as in espaliering onto two supporting wires, spaced 18 and 36 inches off the ground.

After the fruit tree is trained onto the 2 wires, pinch back all lateral shoots early each summer to 4 leaves.

In winter, remove all wood beyond the fruit buds of each spur. Keep the laterals pruned back to 4 leaves until fruit buds form, then cut them off above the fruit buds. Soon the "fence" will be strung with tempting fruit.

Pleaching tree branches

Almost any tree can be pleached but the more supple its branches, the better. Deciduous elms are good subjects. Avoid using evergreen elms (also trees of the genera *Tilia* and *Platanus* and *Laburnum watereri 'Vossii')* because their brittle branches break under pressure as you try to interweave them.

To build an arbor or tunnel by pleaching, you need a framework of vertical and horizontal galvanized pipe to support tree trunks and on which to tie down the overhead branches. The trunks will form the architectural columns; branches trained across the top will create the leafy shelter.

For the simplest arbor, plant a tree next to each of 4 supports that are made of 3-inch galvanized pipes of, say, 12-foot height. The distance between the supports depends on your garden space but we'll assume the supports are 9 feet apart. The overhead trellis should be made of 2-inch pipe, spaced at 3-foot intervals and crossing to make 9 squares.

As the trees grow, remove any vertical growth from the trunks. Bend and tie down branches to the overhead pipe trellis. You can interweave branches together around the support pipes.

Something interesting happens to branches that cross and are tied together: growing together, they help strengthen the network. In several years you will have a canopy of leaves that create a charming, rustic arbor.

Topiary gardens

A garden of unnatural shapes is a concept of the 18th and 19th centuries. Formality and artificiality were often considered "good taste" then. Because today's gardens, too, are subject to currents of fashion, they tend to reflect the rather different tastes of the 20th century.

Still, there is always something worth copying from the past, even in gardening. The old English knot garden, for instance, still seems to be at home in today's landscapes. Perhaps that's because its aromatic shrubs are left rounded and soft. A better guess is that the knot is irresistible in its fragrances.

The knot garden

To create a knot garden, you must find or draw a plan in which the 2 lines of shrubs (or 3, if you are ambitious) interweave in a pleasing pattern.

You can use any low compact bush. Traditionally, fragrant plants of distinguishable colors — such as gray lavender and green rosemary — were the style. Green teucrium and gray thyme are also good choices.

Plant shrubs a foot apart. Cut them down to half to insure a compact, low growth and continue shearing them throughout the spring and summer. Shearing in late fall and winter is dangerous because frost can injure the freshly cut foliage.

The compartments created inside the knot pattern make excellent display beds for flowering plants that will not grow taller than the shrubs. To add fragrance to the garden, you could plant pinks—the early, small form of carnations. When knot gardens were popular, pinks, carnations and dianthus were called "gillyflowers." Shakespeare knew them as that.

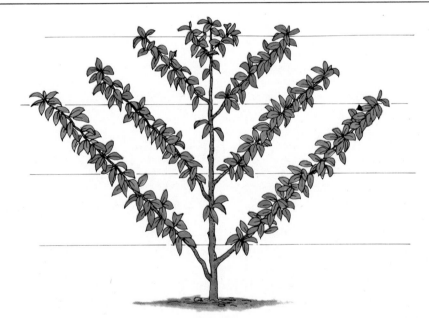

Palmette espalier

Double lattis espalier or
Belgian espalier fence

Parterre

When Catherine de Medici moved from Italy to France to marry King Henry II, she brought along such amenities as ballet dancing, gourmet cooking, a fork to go with the French knife—and the gardening concept of "parterre."

Wealthy Italians had been landscaping their hillside estates with shrubs in patterned lines for over 100 years before this style intrigued the French. But André Lenotre—the 17th Century French landscape architect who designed the gardens at Versailles, Kensington, Fontaineblue and the Vatican—introduced parterre on a grand scale at the French court of Versailles. Here, he planted seemingly endless vistas of shrubs to create geometric patterns. One characteristic of such gardens was pattern reflection—the exact duplication of one side of a design in the opposite side.

A touch of formality can be pleasantly effective in today's gardens if it suits the style of the house. A parterre garden would seem out of place next to a ranch house but appropriate in a traditional setting, such as a French provincial home or one with Georgian architectural lines.

A parterre is constructed much like a knot garden: the chief difference lies in the choice of shrubs. Boxwood serves best but any compact, fine-textured, small-leaf shrub is suitable. Usually green shrubs, such as dwarf holly and teucrium, are chosen for a parterre, but the aromatics—lavender, rosemary, thyme—can also be used.

Parterre compartments can be filled with any low-growing flower or you can do as the French did and lay gravel on the ground between the shrubs. Though gravel will save maintenance, it may also look cold and uninviting.

A collection of topiary

Europe is not alone in its fondness for topiary. In fact, some gardens have been designed around a group of topiaries.

One approach is to place simple cone or sphere topiaries at regular intervals along a green lawn. More elaborately, delightful groups of birds and animals occupy center stage in some topiary gardens.

If an all-out topiary plunge is not for you, the spirit behind such a design can be applied to a simpler formal garden. A single topiary—say, a peacock-shaped yew—in the center of a lawn neatly framed by green or flowering hedges captures the feeling of more elaborate gardens. To many gardeners, this simpler picture is more pleasing just because it is not pretentious. In gardening, too, less can be more.

Whatever your taste, a well-placed, artfully sculptured topiary in a trim garden presents an elegant composition: green sculpture in a green room.

Right: These examples of the green art form from around the world represent just a few of the possibilities. The plants used are yews. ivies. privets and boxwood. among others. Obviously. frequent maintenance is required. The effect. however. is dramatic.

Below: One view of the home of Sir Cecil Beaton in Salisbury. England. The privet topiaries are more than 300 years old.

An Illustrated Glossary

If you see quotation marks within a definition, that term also appears in this glossary.

A

Abscission.
The dropping of leaves or fruit by a plant. Can result from the plant's natural growth process (e.g., fruit ripening) or from external factors (e.g., temperature or chemicals).

Abscission Layer.
Specialized cells, usually at the base of a leaf stalk or fruit stem, that trigger both the separation of the leaf or fruit and the development of scar tissue to protect the plant.

Adventitious.
Growth not ordinarily expected, usually the result of injury or stress. Whereas the plant's normal growth is based on "meristem" tissue (see definition under M), adventitious growth comes from mature nonmeristemic tissue.

Adventitious Bud.
A bud in an unusual place on the plant, often on an "internode." The bud may be a result of an injury. "Suckers" and "water sprouts" usually grow from adventitious buds.

Adventitious Roots.
Ones that occur in an unusual or abnormal place, often where a branch comes in contact with the soil or damp material. A plant cannot be reproduced with cuttings or layering unless adventitious roots develop on them.

Alternate.
Single buds growing at intervals along a stem, one bud at each node. Distinct from "compound," "opposite" and "whorled" buds.

Alternate Bearing.
The characteristic of some fruit plants to bear heavily one year and lightly or not at all the next.

Annual.
A plant that lives only one year or season, then dies.

A

Annual Ring.
The ring in most plants that indicates one year of growth. Annual rings are easily seen in the "traverse cut" of a woody stem or branch

Anvil Pruner.
A pruning tool that cuts a branch between one sharpened blade and a flat anvil-shaped piece of softer metal.

Apex.
The tip of a stem or root.

Apical.
Of or at the apex.

Apical Dominance.
The inhibition by the plant's tip of the dormant buds below it. This is a function of the hormone "auxin" produced by the growing stem apex. Removal of the growing tip increases lateral bud break and subsequent branching, usually directly below the cut.

Arbor.
A structure covered by vines.

Asymmetric.
Unbalanced. One side quite different from the other in size, weight or appearance.

Auxin.
One of the best known and probably most important plant hormones. Most abundantly produced in the actively growing tips of a plant. Generally stimulates growth by cell division in that region and by cell elongation lower down the shoot. Growth of lateral buds is strongly inhibited by the concentrations of auxin that are normal for the growing tip. Artificial auxin is available.

Axil.
The upper angle formed by the stalk of a leaf (the "petiole") with the internode above it on the stem.

Axillary Bud.
A bud that forms in an axil.

B

Ball & Bag,
Ball & Burlap.
A method of preparing a tree or shrub for transplanting. A ball of soil is left around the roots when the plant is dug from the ground and the

ball is wrapped with burlap or a plastic bag to hold it together and retain moisture.

Bare Root.
Another method of transplanting. A dormant tree or shrub is dug up, then its roots are washed, trimmed and kept moist until replanted.

Basal.
At or near the base of a branch or trunk. Sometimes also means at or near the crown of the plant.

Basal Break.
New growth that develops at the base of a branch or near the crown.

B & B.
Common abbreviation for "ball & burlap."

Bearing Age.
The age at which a plant typically bears its first flowers or fruit.

Bleeding.
The exuding of sap from a pruning cut or other wound.

Bole.
Same as "trunk."

Border.
A row of low-growing plants along the edge of a garden. Also, a very narrow, elongated bed of plants.

BR.
Common abbreviation for bare root.

Bract.
A modified leaf, usually small but sometimes large and brightly colored, growing at the base of a flower or on its stalk. Clearly seen on dogwood and poinsettia.

Branch.
A woody extension growing from the trunk or a limb.

B

Break.
Any new growth coming from a bud.

Broad-leaf,
Broad-leaved.
Any landscape plant with wide, flat leaves. Usually used to distinguish broad-leafed evergreens from the conifers which have needlelike leaves.

Brush Out.
The cutting of dead twigs or branches and brush-like growth from a shrub or tree.

Bud.
A small swelling or projection from which a shoot, leaves or flowers develop.

Budding.
The grafting of a bud onto the stock of a different plant. The bud is then the "scion."

Bud Eye.
Another term for bud.

Bud Head.
A swollen or enlarged area where a bud has been grafted to a stock.

Bud Scale.
A modified leaf that forms a protective covering for a bud.

Bud Union.
The suture line where the bud or "scion" has been grafted to a stock. Sometimes called a graft union.

Burl.
Outgrowth of hard wood on a trunk or branch.

Burlapped.
The wrapping of a rootball in burlap to hold it together and retain moisture.

C

Callus.
Scar tissue formed around wounds. Often called callus-roll when referring to healing of larger tree wounds. Formation of callus is greatly aided by a smoothly finished pruning cut. Also, the mass of special cells grown by both scion and stock after grafting. These new cells form the actual joint or union.

Calyx.
All the "sepals" of a flower collectively; the cup, usually green, between the flower and its stem.

Cambium.
The living, growing layer of cells beneath the bark of woody plants.

Candelabra.
A rosarian term for a strong, dominant cane with accelerated growth originating from the bud union that explodes with many blooms.

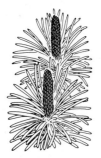

Candle.
New terminal growth on a pine from which needles will emerge.

Cane.
A long vigorous stem, usually of a rose, raspberry, blackberry or similar plant.

Canker.
A place in the bark or wood, usually swollen but sometimes sunken, that indicates decay caused by disease.

Canopy.
The top branches and foliage: the shape-producing structure of a tree or shrub.

Cavity.
A hole or hollow place in bark or wood, caused by decay.

Central Leader.
A trunk or stem extending up through the axis

of a tree or shrub and clearly emerging at the top. Also, a system of pruning that uses the central leader as the basic component.

Chipper.
A machine that reduces pruned-off woody twigs and branches to small chips that are easy to dispose of or use as mulch. Called a "grinder" or "shredder" when applied to greener, softer twigs.

Chlorophyll.
The green pigment in plant tissue that is essential for photosynthesis.

Climber.
Any plant that seeks support by twining, tendrils or rootlike hold fasts.

Clippers.
Pruning or hedge shears that cut with a scissor action.

Columnar.
One of several standard terms used to describe tree forms. A tall, narrow, relatively straight-sided tree or shrub. Lombardy poplar is an example. See "form" for other standard terms.

Compact.
A plant that is relatively short, bushy and has lots of "lateral" branches and foliage. Distinct from "leggy."

Compound Bud.
More than one bud together on the same side of a node. Usually, unless growth is extremely vigorous, only one of the buds breaks and its branch may have a very sharp angle of attachment. If it is removed, a wider-angled shoot is usually formed from the second or accessory bud. Ash and walnut trees typically have compound buds.

Conical.
A tree or shrub with a wide base and pointed top; pyramid-shaped. Fir and spruce are examples.

Conifer.
Cone-bearing trees and shrubs, mostly evergreens. Pine, spruce, fir, cedar, yew and juniper are examples.

Cordon.
A method of espaliering fruit trees, vines, etc. to horizontal, vertical or angled "palmette" wire or wooden supports so a maximum of branch surface is exposed to the

sun, resulting in maximum fruit production. A branch attached to the support is also referred to as a cordon.

Creeper.
A plant with trailing shoots that develop roots along most of their length. Ivy, ice plant and Virginia creeper are examples.

Crosscut.
A cut made at a right angle to the direction of growth. Same as traverse cut.

Crotch.
The angle formed by a main and secondary branch or by a branch and the trunk.

Crown.
The branches and foliage of a tree or shrub collectively. Also the thickened base of a

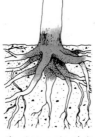

plant's stem or trunk to which the roots are attached.

Cultivar.
A contraction of "cultivated" and "variety." It refers to a named group of plants within a cultivated species that is distinguished by a character or group of characteristics. An example is 'Jonathan' apple or 'Sunburst' locust. Cultivars are propagated asexually and would not survive or reproduce in nature. Note that the name of the cultivar is capitalized and set off with single quotation marks.

Cut.
The act of pruning away a plant part, whether with your fingernails, shears or a saw. Also, the point

on the plant where the removal takes place.

Cutting.
A section of stem or branch that will form adventitious roots. A common method of asexual propagation. A "scion" if used for grafting to a root stock or for propagating by planting. Sometimes called a "slip."

D

DBH.
Common abbreviation for "diameter breast high."

Deadhead.
The act of removing spent flower heads, as from rhododendrons.

Deciduous.
A plant that sheds all its leaves annually. Distinct from "evergreen."

Decurved.
The downward curvature of a branch as it grows.

Deflexed.
The bending down of a branch by the weight of snow, fruit, etc. or by training.

Dehorn.
A drastic method of pruning a neglected tree or shrub. It entails the removal of large branches, especially high in the crown, a few at a time over several seasons.

Delayed Open Center.
A pruning system, usually used on fruit trees, where the tree is pruned to a central leader until it reaches 6 to 10 feet and then pruned with the "open center" system from then on.

Delayed Vase.
Same as "delayed open center."

Deliquescent.
A tree in which the main trunk divides into many branches forming a wide, spreading crown with no central leader. Elm, ash and the *Prunus* species are examples.

Deshoot.
The thinning out of first-year or growing shoots.

Diameter Breast High.
The diameter of a tree 4½ feet above ground level.

Dioecious.
Male and female flowers are on separate individual plants. An example is holly (*Ilex*). If female hollies are to have ber-

ries, male hollies need to be in the vicinity to provide them with pollen. See "monoecious."

Disbud.
Usually used to describe the selective removal of some flower buds so the remaining buds receive more of the plant's energy and become bigger, producing showier flowers. Examples of plants that are often disbudded are roses and camellias.

Dogleg.
A branch that starts out horizontally and then curves sharply upward. A dogleg is usually considered unsightly and removed.

Dormant.
Resting or not growing. A deciduous tree is dormant in winter.

Dormant Bud.
One formed during the growing season that remains quiescent during the winter or dry season that follows. If it does not expand in the next growing season, it is termed "latent."

Dormant Prune.
To prune a plant while it is dormant.

Dressing.
A compound applied to a pruning wound. Also called "pruning paint" or "sealing compound."

Drip Line.
An imaginary line on the ground directly beneath the outermost tips of a plant's foliage. Rain tends to drip from the leaves on this line.

Drop Crotch, Drop Prune.
A type of pruning where a main branch or leader

is removed by cutting to a large lateral—a major crotch is thereby removed or dropped. This term is usually applied to the pruning of large trees.

Dwarf.
A plant that is smaller than the usual ones of its species. Dwarfing is accomplished by selective pruning, controlling nutrients, grafting to a dwarfing rootstock or genetically.

E
Edible.
Plants that are grown for their fruits, nuts, berries, etc. Distinct from "ornamental."

Edible-Ornamental.
A plant that is grown for its appearance but also has edible parts. Plum and blueberry are examples.

Espalier.
The training of a tree or shrub to grow flat on a trellis or against a wall. Espalier patterns may be very precise and formal or more natural and informal.

Evergreen.
A plant that never loses all of its foliage at the same time.

Excurrent.
A tree form in which the main trunk remains dominant with small, more or less horizontal branches. Fir and sweet gum are examples.

Eye.
Another term for bud.

Extension Pruner.
A saw or lopper on a pole or series of poles used to prune high limbs without a ladder.

F
Family.
A more or less natural association of plants categorized together because of a few common resemblances.

Fastigiate.
A tall, very narrow tree or shrub with a strong central leader and all branch attachments at a very acute angle. Italian cypress is an example.

Flower.
A specialized short shoot with leaves modified into sexual (reproductive) structures.

Flower Bud.
A bud that breaks into one or more flowers rather than a shoot.

Flower Truss.
A cluster of flowers, usually compact, growing at a "terminal."

Force.
The intentional directing of growth to a selected bud or branch by the pruning out of other buds or branches.

Form.
The overall shape or habit of a tree or shrub as described in several standard terms. These include "conical," "fastigiate," "globe," "irregular," "pyramidal," "round," "spreading," "vase-shaped" and "weeping."

Formal.
A very regular or orderly arrangement of plants, paths, fences, etc., usually very symmetrical. Also, the precise, smooth shearing of shrubs and hedges. Distinct from informal or natural.

Framework.
The trunk and main branches of a tree or shrub; the basic structure that gives it its shape.

Freeze Damage.
The brown or black withered shoots and buds that have been killed by cold weather.

Frost Cracks.
Cracks in the bark and wood of tender plants caused by extremely cold weather or sudden drop in temperature.

Frost Damage.
Same as freeze damage.

Fruit.
The seed-bearing part of a plant: the mature ovary, including its envelope and any closely connected parts.

G
Genetic Dwarf.
A plant that grows smaller than others of its species naturally, without manipulation. Usually produced by selective breeding.

Genus.
The principal subdivision of a "family." A more or less closely relatable and definable group of

plants comprised of one or more species. The generic name is the first word in a plant's botanical name. The plural is genera.

Geotropism.
The turning or curving of a plant's parts oriented by gravity. Roots growing downward and seed sprouts growing upward are examples. Controlled largely by the hormone "auxin."

Girdling.
The cutting, removing or clamping of the bark completely around a trunk or branch. Sometimes girdling is done deliberately to kill an unwanted tree but often it is the result of natural

feeding habits of some insects and rodents. Wires or ties once used to support the tree can girdle.

Globe, Globular.
A round or oval-shaped crown, usually without a central leader. An ash tree is an example.

Grafting.
The act or method of inserting a shoot or bud of one plant into the trunk, branch or roots of another where it grows and becomes a permanent part.

Grinder.
Same as a "chipper."

H
Hanger.
A drooping branch on a tree that normally doesn't have a drooping or weeping habit. Sometimes, a partially broken branch left hanging.

Hardy.
Frost or freeze tolerant. In horticulture, this term does not mean tough or resistant to pests or disease.

Hat Rack.
An overly long dead end or stub left after a cut.

Head, Head Back.
To cut a stub, a lateral bud or a weak lateral

branch. Usually done to reduce the size of a tree or shrub.

Heading Height.
The optimum height at which a young tree should be headed to stimulate branching. It varies with the species and ultimate use of the tree.

Heartwood.
The oldest wood; the hard central, often deeply colored portion of a tree trunk.

Hedge.
A row of plants, usually of the same kind, trimmed or sheared more or less vertically to form a screen or background in a landscape.

Hedge Shears.
Hand or electric clippers expressly designed to trim and prune hedges.

Herbaceous.
A soft, pliable, usually barkless shoot or plant. Distinct from stiff and woody growth.

Hybrid.
The offspring of two different varieties, species or genera.

I
Informal.
Natural; planted or pruned to let nature more or less have her way rather than in a precise, regimented fashion.

Internode.
The portion of stem between two successive "nodes."

Interstock.
The middle piece when a graft combination is made up of more than two parts; the piece between the "scion" and the "stock." It often has a dwarfing effect. Also called interixitem.

Irregular.
A tree with no regular geometric form.

J
Joint.
A node; the place on a stem where a bud, leaf or branch forms.

K
Knot Garden.
A formal garden in which two or more kinds of plants with different colored foliage are

planted and pruned so they interweave and form a knot pattern. Herb plants are often used.

L
Latent Bud.
A bud that does not break within the season after it's formed. Usually on the lower portion of shoots, it does not expand under normal growth stimuli. Will be stimulated into breaking if the growth above it is damaged or pruned away.

Lateral.
A branch attached to and subordinate to another branch or the trunk.

Lateral Bud.
A bud on the side, rather than the apex, of a stem.

Layering.
A method of stimulating the formation of adventitious roots on a stem by bending the stem and planting part of it to propagate.

Leader.
A developing stem or trunk that is longer and more vigorous than any laterals.

Leaf Bud.
A bud that will produce leaves when it breaks.

Leaflet.
A single division of a compound leaf.

Leaf Scar.
A visible, thickened crescent or line on a node just under the bud where a leaf had been attached.

Leggy.
A plant or stems that have leaves and branches too far apart for a pleasing appearance.

Limb.
Any of the larger branches of a tree or shrub.

Lopper.
A long-handled pruner designed to cut thicker branches than can be cut with hand pruners.

Lower.
To shorten the overall height of a tree or shrub.

M

Modified Central Leader, Modified Leader.
A system of pruning used primarily on fruit trees. The central leader is encouraged for the first few years, then it is gradually suppressed. This system allows for well spaced scaffolds and strong crotches, and at the same time keeps the tree relatively close to the ground for easy harvesting.

Monoecious.
Flowers are either male or female but both occur on the same individual plant. Pecans and avocados are monoecious. See "dioecious."

Mulch.
Any material laid on the soil surface to conserve soil moisture, moderate soil temperature and/or aid in weed control. Wood chips, bark chips and shredded leaves are examples; inorganic materials are also used.

Multiple Crotch.
Where three or more branches join very closely together. A weaker joint than well spaced, wide angled crotches.

N

Node.
The point on a plant where a branch, bud or leaf develops. On younger branches it is usually marked by a slight swelling. The space on the stem between nodes is the internode.

Nodding.
Arching downward. Deodora cedar and many spireas are examples.

O

Open, Open Up.
To thin a tree or shrub to allow more light and air circulation within the crown.

Open Center.
A system of pruning, usually used on fruit trees, where the mature tree will have a short trunk and all the branches spread outward. The center of the tree is open so light can penetrate and encourage fruiting on the lower branches. Also called "vase pruning."

Opposite.
Two buds at a node pointing away from each other. Distinct from "alternate" or "whorled" buds.

Ornamental.
A plant grown only for its appearance in the landscape rather than for a food crop.

P

Palmate.
Term used to describe a leaf that has veins radiating outwards from a single point somewhat like fingers of a hand. Also a form of espalier training.

Parterre.
A formal garden in which the shrubs, flowers and paths form a geometric pattern of matched pairs.

Petiole.
The stalk of a leaf.

Phloem.
The food-conducting tissue of trees and shrubs. The live tissue next to the bark; the inner bark.

Photosynthesis.
The formation of carbohydrates in green plants from water and carbon dioxide by the action of sunlight and the chlorophyll in the leaves.

Phototropism.
A growth response to light. The growth of plant foliage toward or away from light is an example.

Pinch, Pinch Back, Pinch Out.
To head a growing shoot, usually by using just your fingernails as a pruner. Typically, pinching is done to stimulate side growth and form a bushier plant.

Pith.
The soft, central tissue of a stem.

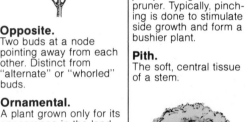

Pleach.
To intertwine branches of trees or shrubs to form an arbor.

Pole Pruner.
A saw, lopper or both fixed on the end of a pole for pruning in hard-to-reach places.

Pole Saw.
A saw on the end of a pole for pruning hard-to-reach places.

Pollard.
To head back severely to main branches of a tree each year so as to produce a thick, close growth of young branches.

Prickle.
A rigid, straight or hooked outgrowth of the bark or stem, often called a "thorn" but not technically the same thing. A rose has prickles.

Prune.
The removal of part of a plant for the benefit of all of the plant — to improve the plant's health,
to increase production of flowers or fruit or to direct growth and improve its appearance or utility.

Pruning Knife.
One made especially for pruning. It usually has a slightly hooked blade that is broader at the tip than at the base.

Pruning Paint.
A special paint for sealing pruning cuts and other wounds usually with an asphalt base. Also called "dressing" or "sealing compound."

Pyramidal.
A tree with a broad base that tapers to a pointed apex; conical-shaped.

R

Radial Spacing.
The relative position of branches around the trunk. Distinct from vertical spacing.

Raise.
To prune so as to increase the overall height of a tree or shrub.

Rambler.
Any plant that grows or spreads in all directions. In particular, certain climbing roses.

Regular.
Uniform in shape or distribution of parts; radially symmetrical.

Renew.
To prune out old wood to buds or newer branches that will fill in and replace what has been removed. Implies severe pruning. Usually refers to fruiting wood.

Renovate.
To reshape or renew a tree or shrub that has been neglected.

Replacement.
A branch that grows from a bud to replace or fill in an area where another branch has died or been removed.

Reversion Growth.
Stems that originate from and have the characteristics of the stock; "suckers."

Ring.
May refer to either "annual rings" or "shoulder rings."

Root Prune.
The cutting or removal of some of a plant's roots. Usually done at the time of transplanting to balance the amount of roots with the amount of foliage. Also done to
plants such as wistaria to promote flowering and to trees where roots are lifting sidewalks or other structures.

Roots.
The underground part of a plant. A primary organ of all landscape plants that serves to anchor the plant to the soil and to absorb water with minerals.

Rootstock.
The root or stem onto which a scion or interstock is grafted.

Rosette.
A small cluster of leaves radially arranged in an overlapping pattern.

Roundheaded.
A tree with a globular or oval crown.

Runaway.
Another term for "sucker" or "water sprout."

S

Scaffolds, Scaffold Branches.
The principal branches of a tree or shrub arising from the trunk or another main branch to form the framework.

Scale.
A modified leaf that protects a bud. Same as "bud scale." Also an insect pest.

Scion.
The cutting or bud of a desired plant that is grafted to the stock of another plant.

Scissor Pruner.
A pruner with two sharp blades that slide past each other as they cut.

Screen.
A row of trees or shrubs, a hedge or vines on a

trellis that are used to provide privacy or concealment.

Sealing Compound.
Another term for "pruning paint" or "dressing."

Sepal.
One of the appendages at the base of a flower, typically green or greenish and more or less leafy in appearance. Collectively, the "calyx."

Shape.
To alter or improve the form of a tree or shrub by pruning.

Shear.
To smooth the surface foliage of a tree or shrub by cutting all the shoots to the same length, as in trimming a formal hedge or topiary.

Shears.
Any of the several kinds. of pruners utilizing two blades or a blade and anvil to make cuts.

Sheath.
A tubular structure, such as a leaf base, that encloses a stem. Also, scabbard in which to carry a pruning tool.

Shoot.
A terminal stem and its leaves collectively.

Shoot Pruning.
The removal of shoots.

Shoulder Ring.
One of the ridges around the base of a branch where it attaches to the trunk or to another branch.

Shredder.
See "chipper."

Shrub.
A woody plant with a number of branches from near the base, usually smaller than a tree.

Side Branch.
Same as a "lateral."

Simple Bud.
A single bud, not one that is compound.

Slip.
Same as a "cutting."

Soft Pinch.
To remove only the succulent tip of a shoot, usually with the tips of the fingers.

Species.
A group of plants closely resembling each other and which interbreed freely.

Spreading.
A tree with a wide-reaching, horizontal branching habit. A Golden-rain tree is an example.

Spur.
On fruit trees, a short, compact twig with little or no internodal development on which flowers and fruit are borne.

Stake.
A system of one or more vertical supports for a tree or shrub. Also, to use such a system.

Standard.
Any plant not naturally growing as a tree that is trained to a single trunk with a globular crown. A tree rose is an example.

Stem.
One of the small branches of trees and shrubs that typically bears the flowers, fruit and leaves. Sometimes also used to refer to the trunk or main stem.

Stipules.
The pair of appendages found on many leaves where the leaf stalk meets the stem.

Stock.
The plant that provides the roots onto which the scion is grafted.

Stolon.
A branch or shoot originating at the summit of a root or from the crown.

Strip.
To remove all the leaves, stems and small branches from a larger branch or the trunk.

Often done to expose the framework of a tree or shrub.

Stub.
Section of branch between a pruning cut and a node. Also, the end of a branch after pollarding or renewal pruning before adventitious growth breaks.

Sucker.
A shoot or stem that originates from the roots or trunk beneath the ground, or from rootstock below the bud head.

Summer Prune.
The shortening of some shoots a month or so before harvest to allow more light and air circulation to reach the ripening fruit.

Sunscald.
The burning of leaves, bark or fruit by overexposure to the sun.

T

Temporary Branch.
One of several small shoots or branches left on the trunk of a young tree for its protection and nourishment. Also, a low lateral that is allowed to remain until a tree is tall enough to have scaffolds at the desired height.

Tender.
A lack of tolerance to frost and cold temperatures. In horticulture, it does not mean weak or susceptible to pests or disease.

Tendril.
A slender projection for clinging, usually a modified leaf. Easily seen on many vines.

Terminal.
The end or apex, usually of a branch or shoot.

Terminal Bud.
The bud at the end of a stem or trunk or at the end of a branch that, when it breaks, extends the growth of the plant.

Thin, Thin Out.
To remove laterals at their point of origin or to shorten a branch by cutting to a lateral that is large enough to assume leadership. Also, the removal of premature fruit.

Thorn.
A sharp-pointed growth arising in the wood of the plant. Sometimes called "prickle" but not technically the same thing. Pyracantha has thorns.

Tip.
The apex or growing point of a shoot or stem.

Tip Prune.
The pruning out of growing tips to stimulate side growth and a bushier plant.

Topiary.
To shape and shear a tree or shrub into an ornamental, unnatural form — usually a geometric shape or the shape of an animal.

Train.
The alteration of the form or size of a plant to improve its appearance or usefulness. May involve removal of plant parts (pruning) to shape or direct growth as well as fastening the plant to a support structure.

Traverse Cut.
Same as a "crosscut."

Tree.
A perennial woody plant, usually having a single main trunk that exceeds 10 feet in height and 2 inches DBH when mature. (Some standard definitions use 15 feet for mature height.)

Trellis.
The structure, usually a latticework of wood or metal, on which vines or creeping plants are trained.

Tropism.
The tendency of a plant part to turn in response to an external stimulus, either by attraction or repulsion, as a leaf turns toward the light.

Trunk.
The main stem or axis of a tree, mostly below the branches.

Truss.
A flower cluster, usually growing at the terminal of a stem or branch.

Twig.
A small stem, often many-jointed, growing laterally to a main stem or branch.

U

Understock.
The plant that provides the root onto which the scion is grafted.

V

Variety.
The lowest major classification of plants — a subgroup with particular like characteristics within a species. Each variety keeps the basic character of the species but

has at least one, sometimes more, individual characteristic of its own. A variety of a species will perpetuate itself in nature. Man-made varieties are developed by crossbreeding the parents of different species: see "cultivar."

Vase Pruning.
A pruning system often used on fruit trees where the mature tree will have a short trunk and all branches spread outward. The center of the tree is left open and "vase-shaped" so light can penetrate to the fruit inside and on the lower branches. Also called "open center" pruning.

Vase-Shaped.
A tree that is narrow at the base of the crown and broadest at the top. The Japanese pagoda tree and American elm are examples.

Vertical Spacing.
The relative position of branches up and down the trunk. Distinct from "radial spacing."

W

Water Sprout.
A vigorous shoot originating above the ground or bud union, from the trunk or older wood. Usually breaks from a latent bud.

Weeping.
A tree with branches or stems that droop or hang down. A Weeping willow is an example.

Whorled.
More than two buds or leaves at each node.

Wood, Woody.
The trunk or any branch from last year's growth or older that has become rigid and has developed a layer of bark. Distinct from "herbaceous" growth.

X

Xylem.
The water-conducting tissue of trees and shrubs.

Index